Dis-empowerment an[illegible]ement

Raising Consciousness

Rev'd. Dr. Robinson A. Milwood. PhD.

TamaRe House

Dis-empowerment and Engagement

Raising Consciousness

Rev'd. Dr. Robinson A. Milwood. PhD.

Published with TamaRe House, October 2010
25 Brixton Station Road, London, SW9 8PB, United Kingdom
044 (0)844 357 2592, info@tamarehouse.com, www.tamarehouse.com

This publication employs acid free paper and meets all ANSI standards for archival quality paper.

A CIP Record of this title is available from the British Library.

ISBN 9781906169-42-8

Books by Dr. Robinson A. Milwood

Pain- Suffering- Persecution:
My Existential-Empirical Journey 1978-2008

The Psychological Combination of Christianity and Slavery

Liberation and Mission: A Black Experience

Suspension: A Testimony of Faith, Suffering and Perseverance

European Christianity and the Atlantic Slave Trade:
A Black Hermeneutical Study

Let's Journey Together

Book Contents

Introduction

The transatlantic (Black African) slave trade or according to Professors Hilary McD. Beckles and Verene A. Shepherd in their eximious 2007 published thesis entitled "Saving Souls The Struggle to End The Transatlantic Trade In Africans" (TTA) has occupied the academic attention of historians for nearly forty years. It is noteworthy that the transatlantic slave trade has not occupied European and British Scholars attentions of Religious Philosophers, Theologians, Sociologists, Educationalists, Anthropologist and Church Historians. However, African-American scholars have engaged themselves in the subject because of their African-American consciousness and shared consciousness-connection of their psychic-connection with slavery and the Middle Passage. Most African-Americans have a deep sense of psychological connection with Africa as a significant part of their connections with the African Kebuka (Middle Passage) Remembering the ancestors through the eye of the Middle Passage and Maafa (The Great Destruction) of the Transatlantic slave trade in Africans.

Caucasian scholars like Prof. David Brion Davis and Prof. Herbert S. Klein from the USA have made considerable seminal academic contributions to the study of the transatlantic slave trade with measured academic rectitude as historians. On the British side Prof. James Walvin is extremely popular. It is necessary to point out that some of Walvin's accounts and elucidations are questionable. They are so, because culturally Walvin is motivated by cultural orientation, rather than the historical dynamism of the literature and historiography. There are many short-comings with Prof. Walvin as a British historian. For example it was late in 2008-2009 that Walvin in the book entitled "The Slavery Reader" edited by himself and Gad Heuman accepted that the transatlantic slave trade was the foundation of European and British economic foundation. He could not have studied comprehensively Dr. Eric Williams egregious contribution with his book Capitalism and Slavery. On the German side, we have the seminal contribution of Prof. Seymour Drescher in his book Abolition A History of Slavery and Antislavery. Previously, British historians had never seen this historical fact as important in the scheme of study. Prof. Roger Anstey (Methodist minister and Historian) at Kent University sought to undermine the contribution of Dr. Eric Williams work in his Capitalism and Slavery. Prof. Anstey also made the postulation in his book (Liverpool, the African Slave Trade, and Abolition) that the brutal enslavement of Africans beyond 500 years was part of God's "Salvation History". I must point out that Prof. Anstey's claim is based on a British endemic culture of mendacity and Racism theologically, historically and philosophically. The Methodist Church asserted that the black race was inherently inferior to whites and they further made the claim with theological justification. Blacks it was alleged were biologically ordained for hard work and slavery.

In a broad survey of the subject it is noticeable that there are specific areas of the transatlantic slave trade that are missed. Areas of importance such as Slaves Rebellions or Resistance, Slaves Revolutions which influenced and impacted on the Abolition Movement and Slaves Narratives. Sometimes these important contributions of the African slaves themselves are not considered as pertinent to the history of the Transatlantic Slave Trade in Africans and the additional importance to a better understanding of what has been made to be a problematic subject. The contributions of Dr. Richard Hart's books (Slaves Who Abolished Slavery. Vols. 1&2. Blacks in Bondage) and The Black Jacobins by C.L.R. James- Toussaint L'Ouverture and the San Domingo Revolution. These are vitally important areas and aspects of the Transatlantic Slave Trade in Africans. The central involvement of the major denominations is another dimension of tremendous importance. The active involvement of the major denominations namely, Catholics, Methodists, Anglicans, Baptists, United Reformed, Quakers and Moravians.

The transatlantic slave trade was a heinous system of racialised slavery enmeshed by these churches theologically with the concept of Infralapsarianism. The slave trade system and the theology in union were morally in the human category of profligacy. It was theologically and sociologically profligate-ness. In other words brutality and extreme racism with wickedness. It was a racist Institution based on European and British Caucasian Christianity without any moral content and moral integrity. It was based on European and British cultural Racism. The Transatlantic Slave Trade in Africans was designed by Europeans and British for the following fundamental reasons. For economic greed and the demonstration of superiority. It was an institution based on white psychic-disconnection or psychic- distance. (Dr. Mary E. Modupe Kolawole) writing on "An African View of Transatlantic Slavery and the Role of Oral Testimony in Creating a New Legacy" she coined and was the first African scholar to have used the term "Psychic-Distance" in relation to the savages from Europe and Britain. It was brutal enslavement of Africans. The institution of slavery was based on the concept of (hegemony) domination, superiority and a white Caucasian God. It was European and British Racism concomitant with economic greed and profits. Christianity for Europeans and British was the driving piston and dynamo of Slavery. It was a cultural outlet based on Racism and nothing whatsoever, to do with liberation and emancipation of the Africans from slavery.

The Cambridge University graduate, Edward Blyden wrote a document entitled, Islam, Christianity and the Negro in 1888. His articulation reads. “No one can deny the great aesthetic and moral advantages which have accrued to the Caucasian race from Christian art, through all of its stages of development, from the Good Shepherd of the Catacombs, to the Transfiguration of Raphael, from rough mosaics to the inexpressible delicacy and beauty of Gioto and Fra Angelico.” But to the Negro, all these exquisite representations exhibited only the physical characteristics of a foreign race; and, while they tended to quicken the taste and refine the sensibilities of that (Caucasian) race, they had only a depressing influence upon the Negro who felt that he had neither part nor lot so far as his physical character was concerned in these splendid representations. A strict adherence to the letter of the Second Commandment would have been no drawback to the Negro. To him the painting and sculpture of Europe as instruments of education had been worse than failures; they have raised barriers in the way of his normal development. They have set before him models of imitation; and his very effort to conform to canons of taste, thus practically suggested, has impaired, if not destroyed, his self-respect and has made him the weakling and creeper when he appears to Christian land.”

Edward Blyden was articulating both the culture and racist perception of his age. The period of the eighteen century or the Enlightenment period was a time of extreme intellectual racism. Hilary McD. Beckles and Verene A. Shepherd have explained this historical fact exceptionally well. For both scholars claimed that “Some European philosophers who spoke and wrote on the question of human liberty, social freedom, justice, and notions of the public good, supported and participated in the TTA. John Locke of England successfully established a reputation as a leading philosopher on the theory of liberty. Yet he was hardly considered compromised by the published evidence of his deep financial involvement in the TTA. Not only was Locke recognized as an authority on human liberty, he was known as a business administrator, and a principal investor in the Royal African Company. In addition he was an investor in the sugar plantation economy of the Bahamas."

Likewise, Thomas Hobbles provided an intellectual legitimization of slavery with his writings on freedom and the social functions of the state. He saw Africans as captives of war defeated in a power struggle by a dominant state. Slavery for both Hobbes and Locke was consistent with modern notions of human liberty.

Voltaire, in particular, rejected the anti-intellectualism of racism, specifically its white supremacy expressions, and ridiculed the idea that a so-called "white race." was entitled to enslave a so-called 'black' race. Voltaire was persistently aggressive in his criticism of the Catholic Church, ridiculing the litany of papal bulls that endorsed the slave system and advocated the rights of whites to dominate others. He regarded it a sign of ignorance that people should consider human features such as skin colour, hair texture, and facial structures important indicators of civilization, and condemned slaves as contemptible for using such arguments in justification of their trade in death". Hilary McD. Beckles and Verene A. Shepherd "Saving Souls, The Struggle to End The Transatlantic Trade in Africans" 2007.

Dr. Runoko Rashidi writing in his "Travel Notes 2005" demolished immediately the Cambridge University graduate Edward Blyden statement based on racism and unscientific verification. Rashide says. "Thousands of years ago the first men and the first women on this planet came out of Africa and they were Black people. Not only were the first people Black, but the people who developed the earliest civilization in the world were also Black people. It is very important that we talk about the achievements of the past so that we can begin to give our people a sense of pride and dignity." Mr. Robin Walker shared the same postulation as Dr. Rashide in his book 'When We Ruled The Ancient and Mediaeval History of Black Civilisations. 2006. Dr. Rashide continued. "At Cape Coast-Elmina I went into the putrid dungeon and saw where my Ancestors were packed in. I visited the female dungeon and saw where my Ancestors were held and raped by their white slave catchers." It is these pagans, heathens and uncivilized British Edward Blyden wrote about above. It is important for historically informed people to remember that European and British systems relating to Africans are based on lies and racism. Edward Blyden and many others like him should visit Egypt's Coptic Museum and see the image of the "Black Christ."

The additional quotation from Dr. Rashide book entitled Travel Notes is helpful in the predication and argument "It was our lot not long ago to hear an illiterate Negro in a prayer meeting in New York entreat the deity to extend his "lily-white hands" and bless the waiting congregation .Another, with no greater amount of culture, preaching from John 3:2, "We shall be like Him", etc. He exclaimed, "Brethren, imagine a beautiful white man with blue eyes, rosy cheeks and flaxen hair, and we shall be like him." The conceptions of these worshippers were what they gathered from plastic and pictorial representations as well as from the characteristics of the dominant race around them."

My academic and intellectual blood is boiling at the blatancy and mendacity of Edward Blyden's statement which is typical of many British scholars. I sat as a B.D. degree student reading "Church History". The subject was the "Early Church Fathers." The course curriculum and the lecturer did not made very clear that the Patristic Fathers and Early Church Fathers were Africans. Rather they were presented by the lecturer as Europeans. Quoting relevantly from the dynamic African-American scholar Dr. Runoko Rashidi Travel Notes: "At the time that the twelve African Christian martyrs died in A.D. 180 there were living two great African personages: Septimius Severus, who later became Emperor of Rome; and Tertullian, one of the greatest of Church leaders." J.C. DeGraft- Johnson, African Glory.

Here is a valid quote from Dr. Rashidi "Ancient African people, sometimes called Moors, are known to have had a significant presence and influence in early Rome. African soldiers, specifically identified as Moors, were actively recruited for Roman military service and were stationed in Britain, France, Switzerland, Austria, Hungary, Poland and Romania. Many of these Africans rose to high rank. Lusius Quietus, for example, was one of Rome's greatest generals and was named by Roman Emperor Trajan (8-117 C.E.) as his successor. Quietus is described as a "man of Moorish race and considered the ablest soldier in the Roman army."

At the end of the second century of the Christian Era more than one third of all of the members of the Roman Senate were born in Africa and Africans were dominant in Rome's intellectual life."

I also knew, regarding the African presence in early Rome, about saints and theologians and martyrs like Tertullian, Cyprian and Augustine.

Quintus Septimius Florens Tertullian, for example was the first of the church writers to make Latin the language of Christianity. Tertullian was born into a rich family in Carthage in 170 C.E. He wrote Greek and Latin fluently and was well trained in the school of rhetoric where Apuleius (another African) had been a pupil a generation before. Tertullian's wife was a Christian and he himself a convert. A man of fiery temperament and evangelical spirit.

There were at least three African Popes at Rome. St. Victor became the first known African bishop of Rome in189 C.E. and reigned until 199 C.E. St. Victor 1, the first Pope to write in Latin and the first Pope known to have had dealings with the imperial household, is described as "the most forceful of the 2nd century." Pope St. Miltiades, a Black priest from Africa, was elected the thirty-second Pope after St. Peter in 311 C.E. The evidence is abundant for us. None of these names in the lecture was ever mentioned to the class as having any African connections.

Most scholars today have not paid enough attention to the (1) Under-development of Africa and the impact of the reiteration legacies of slavery on Africa. It was Dr. Walter Rodney in the 70's who made a significant contribution in his book "How Europe Under-developed Africa." Dr. Rodney's contribution has been ignored by many white scholars. (2) Disempowerment and Powerlessness has been the central programme of Europe, Britain and America's approval and approach to the slave trade. (3) The sociological and psychological impact of slavery on Africa has not seen any serious study. The Dis-empowerment of the black race is a major political, Educational and Economical problem. The Diasporas, Sociological and Psychological historical linage are intertwined. These are central components of the transatlantic (Black African) slave trade history. They must be unblocked by Black people. It is a collective

Diasporas urgent desire and demand especially where there is a measure of intellectual orientation and consciousness. The application must be the breaking of the psychological chains of slavery and the urgency for African political unification. The movement must therefore be one of a determined Pan-Africanism by Africans themselves in conjunction with the African Diasporas.

Dis-empowerment is fundamental to the study of the transatlantic slave trade history. But dis-empowerment and engagement of the slaves (Diasporas) is functional as the two had been in great oscillation throughout the long history of the transatlantic slave trade in Africans. Another appropriate aspect is the great importance which has been placed on the Quakers, William Wilberforce, Thomas Clarkson, Thomas Buxton and Granville Sharpe. The Enlightenment period and the Evangelical Movement The Humanitarian Self-interest of Britain. Britain Industrial Revolution. These had been made by Europeans and British for the purpose of diversion from the historical facts of Black history. At the same-time white scholars ignored and offered very little attention to the immortal Slaves Rebellions leaders both male and female leaders. When slave leaders are mentioned they do not get adequate and substantive elucidations appreciatively. Great paradigms like, Nanny of the Maroon, Harriet Jacobs, Frederick Douglas, Sam Sharpe, Nat Turner, Tacky and Paul Bogle and Toussaint L'Ouverture. Albert James Ukawsaw Gronniosaw, Adam Potkay, Sandra Burr, Cugoano, Quobna Ottobah, Olaudah Equiano, Mary Prince, Ignatius Sancho and Phillis Wheatley, Tomboy of Antigua, Pompey of Exuma Island, Black Tom, Takyi, Blackwall of Jamaica, and Sandy of Tobago.

In this thesis I have embraced the positive engagements of slave leaders, Slave Narratives written by slaves, and the slaves themselves in their struggles for their manumission and emancipation. It is for this reason that I have just listed above those immortal paradigms and historical Black icons. The effectiveness of the slave leaders and their rebellions dictated the time-table (Chronology) for their liberation and emancipation. But there was a great paradox of the transatlantic slave trade in Africans. It was the paradox of Abolition of the Slave trade and the Abolition of slavery; one school of proslavery and the other school of antislavery. Intellectually, scientifically and autobiographically the struggles were gigantic. The moral and theological point is the historical fact that the slaves had no reparation or indemnification from Europe, the USA and Britain. What has been overlooked by scholars, is that the subject of Reparation cannot be made valid without the incorporation of all the major Churches. Political hegemony and Christianity were twins. The denials of reparation and indemnification to the slaves have impacted on Africa and the Diasporas to the present day. The slave trade and semantical cultural Christianity retarded the advancement of Africa. Nicholas Draper in his 2009 publication The Price of Emancipation-Slave-ownership, Compensation and British Society at the end of Slavery with academic explication informed us how the £20,000.000. British compensation was systematically paid to the merchants, enslavers and in particular the Archbishops, Bishops and ministers of religion. The compensation is a clear indication and indictment of the churches deep involvement in the brutal enslavement of Africans for 500 years. The juxtaposition is correct in this paragraphically connection that Prof. Diarmaid MacCulloch in his academic seminal tomb A History of Christianity 2009 made the point of the biblical and historical connection between blackness and slavery. Prof. Mac Culloch says, “That in the fifteenth century, a celebrated Portuguese Jewish philosopher, Isaac ben Abravanel suggested that Canaan’s descendants were black, while those of his uncles were white, and so all black people were liable to be enslaved. Gen.9 gives no support to this belief. Gen.4.1-16.according to this Syriac take on the biblical text, black people actually descended from Cain because when God had punished Cain for killing his brother Abel, the 'mark' he gave the murderer was to blacken his skin." It is remarkable to note that the enslavement of Africans was historically based on European and British Racism, Economic greed, cultural superiority, exploitation and political hegemony.

It is important for me to show the significance of Dis-empowerment and Engagement and the Raising of Consciousness. The slaves had been stripped of their human power and dignity through slavery. Two fundamental forces dominated the lives of slaves for 500 years. They are both physical and psychological. Namely, Excortication and Deracination. Both forces became traumatic syndromes during and after slavery. The impact and formation is what I have postulated as the reiteration legacies. This exogenously created the stream of traumatic syndromes for the slaves. The slaves engagements on the other hand were the only attributes they had between life and death. Prof. David Beck Ryden, Richard Sheridan, and Vincent Brown have drawn our attention to the physical and psychological reduction of the slaves through punishments. While Dr. Joy Leary and Dr. NA'IM Akbar focused on the psychological effects and the traumatic destructions of the slaves. The physical, psychological and spiritual were central in the scheme and philosophy of domination by the enslavers. The application and effectuation is in the different degrees of impacts for the Diaspora and the Continent of Africa. Permanent dis-empowerment of the Africans was the slave traders and enslavers philosophy. It was to be seen as the psychological, economical, political and sociological creation of permanent-powerlessness for the Black race. The delineation and manifestation was to be effective economically, intellectually, scientifically, technologically and politically. But the engagement of the Diasporas and the movement of the rules of the game has changed. Engagement of Africa through the Pan-African Movement and the Diasporas is imperative for a radical quest for empowerment and the psychological feeling of improvidence which has become endemic among Africans and the Diasporas.

It is a fundamental mistake to see the transatlantic slave trade as historically a past event or according to some white scholars as a phenomena. Those whose postulations are, that it is a past event, are not aware of the fact that you cannot separate the past from the present and the present from the future. Africans and African-Caribbean Diasporas share a psychic- connection with the slave trade. It is more dangerous when Africans say it is past or West Indians. To say it is past is significant to the whole moral concept of under-development of Africa and the creation of a symbiotic psychological connection of the Diasporas. It cannot be the past because Africans and the Diasporas live with the daily reiteration legacies of the transatlantic slave trade. The transatlantic slave trade legacies are existential and empirical for all Africans and Diasporas. The psychological and sociological maafa ie destructions are evident within the Black race context.

It is scientifically and psychologically attested by scholars that elephants do suffer from traumatic syndromes. This is more pronounced in countries where elephants are killed frequently. The death of a mother or adult elephant leaving young dependable elephants to grow without the protection and guidance of the adults does create serious traumatic syndromes among the young. The traumatic syndromes are evident reiterations of the transatlantic slave trade syndromes among Africans and the Diaspora. Dr. Joy Leary made the connection between the traumatic experience of elephants and some segment of the African-American community. In the language of globalization technology and economic empowerment the African descendants are conspicuously powerless.

I have spontaneously allocated some attention to Pan-Africanism and I have made my differences quite clear. Pan-Africanism is philosophically and pragmatically an attempt to create the equilibrium between Dis-empowerment-Engagement and Empowerment. The historical approach has been made without radicalization of the psychological attitudes and impact on Africa and the Diasporas. There needs to be acknowledgement that Africa has not begun psychologically, sociologically and politically to dissipate some of the reiteration legacies of the transatlantic (Black African) slave trade mentality. One such legacy is economic improvidence. Africa is constantly looking to Europe, Britain and the USA for charity and massive IMF Loans with interests that will take generations to repay. This attitude is endemically linked to the slave trade. Secondly, under-development is basically a paradox and a product of the transatlantic slave trade in Africans. Africa has not progressed significantly because of the external economical, technological, forces. There is a deep rapscallion endemic culture within the African political environment and society. Most African leaders help themselves, families and friends. The country or people are left with economic crumbs. Hence, Africa is her own enemy. This is where the influence and contributions of the Diaspora comes into full play to effectuate radical psychological and cultural reorientation. The whole African political mindset is in need of urgent mutability.

I have been seriously critical in this thesis on Dis-empowerment and Engagement principally because it is imperative for Africa and the

Diasporas to begin to move drastically and radically away from the transatlantic slave trade mentality and colonial culture of dependency on Europe, Britain and the USA. The continent of Africa is inundated with economical natural resources. But at the same-time Africa lacks technological development. Political unification, Pan-Africanism philosophy and symbiotic will. The West and China are taking control of Africa's resources for their economical expansions. An African company would not be allowed to enter, France, Germany, England or the USA freely to conduct Oil exploration, de-forestation or general expeditions. Yet today China is in Africa big time. The transatlantic slave trade in Africans have depleted Africa demographically, geographically, sociologically and psychologically. Africa is continuing to experience depletion and under-development because of the lack of technology, science, industrialization, political- unification. It is the African philosophy of unity. Africa needs indigenisation economically, educationally, politically and scientifically.

I have looked at Reparation and Memoralization as sources of consciousness and education for Africa and the Diasporas. I have put forward a number of radical suggestions. The most imperative ones are:

1) Psychological connections.

2) Psychological consciousness

3) Protection of Africans Legacies in autobiographical and historical literatures.

4) Immortalization of Africa's Sons and Daughters as Paradigms for

inspiration and emulations .In the African idiom it is called Kebuka. That is “Remembering the ancestors through the eye of the Middle Passage.”

5) Preservation of Slaves Dungeons and Barracoons especially in West Africa (Ghana) and Nigeria and Jamaica.

Inspiration can be drawn paradigmatically from historical figures like Olaudah Equiano, Ignatius Sancho, Frederick Douglas, Harriet Jacobs, Tacky, Nat Turner, David Brown Cudjoe, Coffi, Sam Sharp, Paul Bogle etc. These African sons and daughters have contributed significantly to the Abolition Act of transatlantic slave trade in Africans. Nanny of the Maroon and Cato Mungro are parallel historical figures like Phillis Wheatley, John Marrant, Jupiter Hammon, James Albert Ukawsaw Gronniosaw.. I have sought carefully to circumvent writing a critique of white scholars askance in scholarship. I had to correct Prof. James Walvin. His argument was far too blatant and lambent in overlooking the great contributions of slave leaders of rebellions which historically dictated a positive time-table for abolition and the chronology for the termination of the heinous transatlantic slave trade in Africans. At the same-time I have exposed the evilness of European and British Christianity that was based on a theology of Infralapsarianism viz a theology of the elect and the damned by God. Likewise the Missionary Movement and the churches perceptions of Africans as biologically inferior. That it was necessary to enslaved Africans in order to offer them Christianity. The Methodist missionary minister Rev’d. Dr. Thomas Coke in his book History of the West Indies (1808-1811) claimed that God created Africans in order that whites should impart Christianity to them. Thomas Coke epitomized the missionary philosophy and ideology of Britain’s transatlantic slave trade in Africans expansionism with missionary ideology. "And yet it is to the gospel, that Great Britain, in all probability, stands indebted for the preservation of many of her richest colonial possessions". Helen Thomas Romanticism and Slave Narratives Transatlantic Testimonies. In other words evangelization and Christianization were hands in gloves in the enslavement of Africans. Further-more the major engine of the slave trade was the rapid spread of Christianity by the Churches. But this Christianity was based on European and British paganism and heathenism. Fundamentally, it was based on extreme Racism, oppression and exploitation of Africans through the transatlantic slave trade in Africans. They were attached to the hegemony of Europe and Britain in the economic exploitation of Africa and the brutal psyche- distance of the enslavement of Africans based on racism and economic industrialization of Britain and the under-development of Africa according to the late Dr. Walter Rodney. (How Europe Under-developed Africa)

I have expressed my opinion without reservation that Africans and the Diasporas are a fractured community that needs healing. As a consequence, the black race is dysfunctional, without psychological equilibrium and suffering from paralysis. The Diasporas is a stranded community of African descendants. The healing has a significant process and remedy, but it cannot be effective in ignorance .The slaves at the end of the transatlantic slave trade according to Dr. Eric Williams in his magnum opus book "Capitalism and Slavery" were left in a state of complete ignorance and backwardness. I add to Dr. William's postulation that the slaves were left in a state of destitution, economic dependency and worst of all, the slaves were abandoned in a state of psychological powerlessness. It was the culmination of the pre-planned strategy of enslavement to guaranteed permanent powerless-ness of Africa and African-descendants. The mutant process must be social, political, educational and psychological process of African transformation. Knowledge is power, knowledge is empowerment and engagement. Knowledge of the past namely the transatlantic slave trade history in Africans. Mwalimu K. Bomani Baruti in "Kebuka" (Remembering the Middle Passage Through the Eyes of our Ancestors) made the profound claim that Africans and the Diasporas must encounter that level of psychological connection. It is from this psychological connection that the pregnancy of raising the consciousness, the consciousness-connection will give the birth of solidarity and political unification. The knowledge through information of the great ancestors. Their sufferings and oppressions. The healing process must have the abridgement of Weeping and Mourning. Black people have not mourned for the 500 years of enslavement. In addition the 280,000.000 – 300.000.000 who died during the heinous slave trade in Africans. The Reiteration legacies will not terminate without that imperative weeping and mourning. With the reiteration legacies there is the existential and empirical encounters. Many African-Americans on entering Cape Coast- Elmina dungeon constantly wept openly. This is part of the healing process. But most Africans and the Diasporas have not yet start their weeping. I am using the terminology "weep" to mean the painful process of awareness and consciousness. The process of conscious connection. In addition there is the process of psychological and spiritual connection. These are areas of pertinence to the healing process.

The transatlantic slave trade in Africans was barbaric, heinous racism with mental hatred and heartlessness with psychic-distance by the European and British Churches. The Churches were the central engine and involvement in the horrendous transatlantic slave trade-placed. Europeans and British Churches through their cultural-semantical Christianity should now be placed under a moral mirror. The Churches white Christianity and Theology was without any measured edification. It is definitely efficacious for Black Theology, Liberation Theology and Black scholars (Historians) to apply hermeneutical evaluation and interpretation of the historical and contemporary context and experience of Black people. I add anxiously that white theology and philosophy of religion must undergo radical de-colonization theologically.

African-descendants Traumatic Syndromes

Dr. NA IM Akbar an African- American scholar developed in his book "Breaking the Chains of Psychological Slavery" the concept of "historical trauma" among African-Americans. Second is the "Traumatic Syndrome" which is psychological and is traceable to the transatlantic slave trade in Africans. Dr. Akbar's concepts are tremendously impressive and is compulsive reading for African Diasporas.

Dr. Joy Leary another African American in her book "Post Traumatic Slave Syndrome" followed Dr. Akbar contiguously. Her significant departure from Dr. Akbar is her existential and empirical approach. I am deeply inspired by both of these scholars and I am indebted to both of them. They have motivated me to look and to study carefully the various stages and effects of slavery on the slaves. I have discovered during this forensic hermeneutic research that the slaves experienced many traumatic syndromes. These traumatic syndromes are integral aspects of the Reiteration Legacies of the transatlantic slave trade syndromes caused by 500 years of brutal and horrendous enslavement of Africans juxtaposed between the churches and the hegemony of Europe and Britain based on Racism, economic greed and exploitation of the people called Africans.

The most amazing findings are those affecting the African-Diasporas psychologically, theologically (spiritually) sociologically and culturally. I have called these legacies the "Reiteration Legacies" of the transatlantic (Black African) slave trade. Or transatlantic slave trade in Africans.

My daughter Chrystal has insisted that the terminologies I used to describe and to define the traumatic syndromes are mainly esoterical technical terminologies. That I should endeavour to simplify them without loosing their meanings and impacts. So where I am forced to obey my daughter, I have sought to keep as far as possible from esoterical technical terminologies to exoterically consciously simplified elucidations and vocabulary. In addition I have to make a confession that in my previous thesis on the "Psychological Combination of Christianity and Slavery" The impact on African-Caribbean Psyche. I have developed the concepts of Psychological Randomization Traumatic Syndrome. Suboptimization Traumatic Syndrome, Stultification Traumatic Syndrome and Routinization Traumatic Syndromes. From these early discoveries I have moved on to discover in the research for this thesis, traumatic syndromes such as the following:

Suboptimization Traumatic Syndrome
Randomization Traumatic Syndrome
Routinization Traumatic Syndrome
Dungeonization Traumatic Syndrome
Villagization Traumatic Syndrome
Barracoonization Traumatic Syndrome
Infibulation Traumatic Syndrome
Pummelization Traumatic Syndrome
Stultification Traumatic Syndrome
Deracination Traumatic Syndrome

Infralapsarianism Traumatic Syndrome

Dysfunctionalization Traumatic Syndrome

Imbrications Traumatic Syndrome

Infanticidezation Traumatic Syndrome

Excortication Traumatic Syndrome

Propinquity (propinquus) Traumatic Syndrome

Vilification Traumatic Syndrome

Degradation/ Aggradations Traumatic Syndrome

Middle-Passage Traumatic Syndrome

(African Hellacaust) Kebuka and Maafa

Readers may find some of these post traumatic syndromes and the associated impacts of noci-association shocking and painful to read and especially to comprehend. These will enable you to begin to understand how much Africans and Diasporas are truncated, stunted and fractured. Only Africans and the Diasporas can heal themselves. It is a collective struggle and process. It is a psychological and psychic-connectional healing process. Healing is the revelation of the historical truths. Truths that are not polluted and diluted. Truths that will be painful but the pain is vitally important for the healing to be effective, transformational and sobering. The major healing process is profound knowledge of the history of the transatlantic slave trade in Africans. As an historical subject of paramount importance the transatlantic slave trade in Africans should be a compulsive subject in Primary School, Secondary School, Six Form College and Universities.

The birth of a child is very painful but the joy is the actual child. Any new life cannot be effective from the pit of ignorance but by facing up-to the harsh realities of the heinous crimes of slavery imposed and impacted on African-descendants throughout the Diasporas.

There is one specific journey that all Africans and Diasporas should make their Mecca in life and that is the journey to "Cape Coast Castle" Elmina Castle West Africa. To see the dungeons under-ground where 1000 men, women and children were kept up-to two months in faeces without any ventilation. At the top of the dungeon there is the Catholic Church Communion Table. There they celebrated the Eucharist. Next is the Dutch Reformed Church with the bold inscription "God is in this Place". And on the other-side, the Methodist Church, Baptist Church, United Reformed Church and the Angelican Church. They were all pagans. They were Churches with very, very evil and wicked people. In other words the Churches were a profligate aggregate body. They were there with a profound sense of "Psychic-Distance" They were there making the affirmation of the incongruity of slavery and Christianity. They were affirming Slavery and Christianity. Dr. Walter Rodney's observation is pertinent. Writing on Racism in Caribbean Slavery in the Atlantic World he said the "racism of Europe was a set of generalisations and assumptions, which had no scientific basis, but were rationalised in every sphere from theology to biology. How else can one explain the fact that the Christian church participated fully in the maintenance of slavery and still talked about saving souls. The hypocrisy reached its highest levels inside the U.S.A. The first martyr was an African descendant, Crispus Attucks; both slaves and free Africans played a key role in Washington's armies. And yet, the American Constitution with its famous preamble that all men are created equal sanctioned the continued enslavement of Africans". According to Prof. Verene A. Shepherd in her book Saving Souls said, "when Thomas Jefferson wrote the first draft of the American Declaration of Independence, few people knew that he had fathered children with an enslaved woman, but most had accepted that the TTA had become part of the American way of life. His reference to the sacred rights of life and liberty were not meant to apply to the thousands of Africans within his private or public spaces."

In 2009 Anderson Cooper of the CNN made a report on Cape Coast Castle after President Barack Obama's visit to Ghana. His report revealed that the floor of the dungeon where slaves lived, that even I stood on was covered with over 12ins of faeces formed like concrete over-time. Cape Coast is deeply educational, spiritual psychological-connection with the souls and spirits of the African men, women and children who died in the dungeon and in The Door of No Return. Those who survived and were carried away in the transatlantic Middle Passage to the United States, Brazil, Canada, North America and the Caribbean, their souls and memories must have memorialisation. It is a moral historical significance and requires political responsibility of African leaders. The African Union annual holiday in May should be a time for the call and challenge for Political Unification and a collective moral appeal to Europe, Britain and the US for reparation. Five hundred years of brutal enslavement of Africans. It is incumbent for collective Africans and the collective Diasporas to embark on a moral crusade for reparation.

Women were abused physically, sexually, morally, spiritually and emotionally beyond vocabulary description. Men, women and children were sodomonized. The present revelation of Child Abuse in the Catholic Church in April 2010 is nothing new. It is rather endemic in the culture of the church historically. In a procacious way I have given some meaningful attention to women disempowerment and engagement in the transatlantic slave trade institution. It is not an area of the transatlantic slave trade in Africans that anyone can seek to polemicize. Finally, the traumatic syndromes I have revealed are new forensic hermeneutics in the transatlantic slave trade in African study. They are therefore ground-breaking discoveries. There are much more studies needed especially in the sociological, theological and psychological impact of slavery on the collective mind of Africa. Here the Diasporas must be included in any scheme of research study

The destitute conditions of the slaves when “racial slavery” was recognised as un-economical became of polemical importance politically in the eighteen century. The attempt at de-legalization of the institution of slavery motivated my Mohandas Karamchand Ghandi. The slave traders, merchants, planters and enslavers were compensated by Britain with the payment of £20 million. Payments were made mainly to the Archbishops, Bishops and ordained ministers. The medical slave trade doctors were included. It is what Prof. Davis called “pragmatic necessity.”

The legal administration was the “Compensation Commission” academically articulated by Nicholas Draper in his 2010 publication “The Price of Emancipation” Slave-ownership, compensation and British Society at the End of Slavery. The slaves received no compensation or indemnification. The slaves were left naked, in a state of indigence, victual-less, powerless, stripped, raped, sodomonized and abandoned to condemnation. They were left to face grim poverty, rejection and further dis-empowerment. The slaves were confronted only by their post traumatic syndromes and an un-chartered future. This degree of condemnation is a further in-dite-ment on the character of Europeans and the British with Racism based on Infralapsarianism which was a theology of the elect and the condemned by God. The missionaries, enslavers, merchants and churches saw no incongruity between Christianity and the brutal enslavement of Africans. Indeed, for Prof. Roger Anstey this brutal enslavement of Africans was part of God's Salvation History. Prof. Roger Anstey and many others like him are the re-incarnation of the Dark Ages. Prof. Seymour Drescher in his book "Abolition A History of Slavery and Antislavery" reminds us of the nature of brutality the slaves endured. The suppression of rebellion involved some of the traditional methods of enacting rituals of punishment so terrifying "that no slave would ever dare try it again". Prof. David Beck Ryden following contiguously Dr. Vincent Brown "Spiritual Terror and Sacred Authority in Jamaican Slave Society, Slavery and Abolition" and Dr. Richard Sheridan (Doctors and Slaves: A Medical and Demographic History of Slavery in the British West Indies 1860-1834". This included exemplary executions of individuals chosen at random, decapitating them, and placing their heads on poles along the roads". Dr. Ryden says "Recent historians have emphasised the importance of physical and psychological punishment in organizing Jamaica's slave society. Vincent Brown, for example, outlines the attempts by the white community to inflict 'spiritual terror' on the entire slave population." " To this end, the government sanctioned not only brutal punishment on the living and the condemned, but also the mutilation of slaves corpses in order to prevent slave suicides, an apparent problem among the recently arrived 'new negroes' who hoped to spiritually return to Africa by taking their own lives." Further elaboration on the subject of punishment for physical and psychological reasons reads. "This asymmetry in treatment drove a psychological and social wedge into the slave community, which was key to the maintenance of white domination. It is evident that sadistic tortures were also at the heart of white hegemony." In Burnard's words it was "the fatalism or even levity toward death, which arose from living in a society with a high mortality rate that cultivated white tyranny to unimaginable levels". Bernard recounts the process of breaking slaves both physically and mentally.' A favourite punishment of Thistlewood's was what he called 'Derby's dose', in which the slave was flogged, salt pickle, lime juice and bird pepper were rubbed into the open wounds, and then another slave defecated in his mouth. He was immediately put in a gag whilst his mouth was full and made to wear the gag for four to five hours." Dr. Ryden conclusion is germane and conducive here. "Ultimately, many slaves were so psychologically damaged from the arbitrary power held by their master that they responded to physical punishment with no outward sign of discomfort." I will continue to pose both the theological and philosophical question "Does God Exist?" It is significant to note that the rebel slaves linked their enslavement to their Christianisation. Black Theology and Black Liberation Theologians must, I reiterate re-interpret White Theology because White Theology is based on a culture of Racism, (rather extreme racism) profligacy, oppression, exploitation, economic rapacity, cultural superiority and most importantly White Theology is based on 500 years of Racial-brutal-enslavement of Africans in the name of a White Almighty God- A White-Semantical –Christianity and a White Jesus Christ. The summation of the transatlantic slave trade was the expression of European and British extreme-racism expressed through the rapid spread of Christianity through the agent-Churches. It was a system of flagitiousness in the guise of Christianity with theological justification. (Infralapsarianism) Black Theologians, Black Historians, Black Psychologist, Black Sociologist, Black Philosophers and many others have a tremendous task ahead. The journey philosophically is long but the imperative is the collective first step. My contribution in this thesis is significant to the journey and process by virtue of "Raising Consciousness". I hope many lives and minds will become impregnated and fecund by my thesis and contribution. It is hoped thereby to bring about some measure of positive and effective awareness for the psychological, sociological, theological and economical empowerment of black people and the overdue redress of reparation from governments in Europe, Britain and the USA and all the major Churches.

Dr. Robinson A. Milwood. July 2010

Preface

The Transatlantic Slave trade has become for some white scholars of history an academic fascination without any meaningful cultural, historical or psychological attachment or even psychic- connection. The study of the slave trade is based on systematic documentation provided by the officials and merchants of the institution of the heinous crime of racial slavery. Historians have failed to elucidate hermeneutically the documentations, the philosophy, the theological purpose and claims of the churches for the forceful enslavement of Africans for 500 years. This would include the economic philosophy behind the slave trade institution.

I have decided to research the transatlantic (Black African) slave trade institution historically for the purpose heuristically to unearth the impact and implication of slavery on Africa as a Black continent. Particularly since 1884-85 when the Berlin Conference met and dislocated and truncated Africa into 53 countries within the geographical and demographical African Continent. I am very intrigued at the challenges to find out the psychological, theological and sociological impact of the transatlantic slave trade on Africa demographically, anthropologically, historically, politically, economically, theologically, sociologically and psychologically. For this reason I have used the methodology of "forensic hermeneutic indagation" study of the slave trade.

The beginning of any project is significant to the development of the subject in hand, especially because the development will lead to a positive outcome philosophically, theologically, politically and pragmatically. I began by studying and writing a thesis on European Christianity and the Atlantic Slave Trade published in 2007. I then studied and wrote a thesis on the Psychological Combination of Christianity and Slavery published in 2009. In this present thesis I am concentrating on Dis-empowerment and Engagement-Raising-Consciousness. Taking into account also slavery. Here I am occupied with disempowerment and contextual engagement of Africans and the Diasporas. The Diasporas is vitally important for Africa today and for the future development of Africa as a whole. The Diasporas are not commercially targeted in the scheme of Tourism and development in order to encourage the global Diasporas to re-connect with Africa. Re-connection will be very difficult because there is a tremendous hiatus and heterogeneity psychologically and culturally between Africa and the Diasporas. Intellectually and culturally there is a great need for the Diasporas to learn how to re-connect with Africa. The challenge is imperative because most of the Diasporas are educated negatively about Africa. Africa therefore, politically, culturally, sociologically and psychologically has a massive task. The immediate task is to create and project a congenial, progressive, positive, collectively- connected and receptive Africa for the Diasporas. It is a dynamic programme and ambition.

Dis-empowerment and Engagement has been a great challenge especially in exposing the mythological twists of many scholars. Pan-Africanism is a concentration aspect of this thesis. I have arranged Pan-Africanism and Diasporas critically with memorialisation and reparation by governments in Europe, Britain and the US.

Readers will encounter a number of penetrative psychological, emotional and spiritual Traumatic Syndromes in the thesis. These are made and presented centrally to encourage the intellectual power towards a greater understanding and un-locking of recondite areas of the transatlantic (Black African) slave trade in Africans which was sustained politically and theologically by the churches.

My thesis is not a sublime dissertation but should it achieve the name and appreciation of a ground-breaking thesis I should be pleased. However, it will be more pleasing if the readers find some measure of inspiration and rapacious appetite to delve deeper into the transatlantic slave trade in Africans history as a result of this thesis on Dis-empowerment and Engagement. Raising Consciousness. Women received special appreciation rightly from me. Many accounts are made of male audacious slaves and their great contributions and successful rebellions which the enslavers tried not to report accurately. Throughout the slave trade in Africans, the contributions of women were prodigious and extraordinary. I have shown clearly how slavery was based on European and British Racism and economic rapacity. Here I differ from Dr. Eric Williams where he claimed that racism was not the result of slavery but the cause of slavery. Dr. William was afraid to postulate audaciously that the fundamental basis of slavery was racism. Economic domination, cultural superiority and a theology based on (Infralapsarianism) a theology without any moral content and moral integrity. A theology promulgated by European and British Pagans and to give themselves justification for the brutal enforced enslavement of Africans. Their theology and enslavement of Africans was a pestiferous and profligate crime against the African Monotheistic concept of God and humanity.

The Anglican church openly had their slave plantations in the Caribbean.

The Methodist Church claimed doctrinally and theologically with justification that Black people were biologically inferior to whites. John Wesley, Thomas Fowell Buxton, George Fox, Joseph Surge, Josiah Wedgwood, Joseph Woods, James Phillips, Joseph Hooper, John Barton, Richard Phillips, George Harrison and Samuel Hoare were regarded as influential voices in the campaign of the Society for the Abolition of the Slave Trade. Granville Sharp and Thomas Clarkson must be included. However, in 1774 John Wesley published a pamphlet entitled Thoughts Upon Slavery elucidating his approach to slavery. The pamphlet was literally and utterly a plagiarism of an American scholar. Helen Thomas in her book Romanticism and Slave Narratives Transatlantic Testimonies made the critique observation that Rev. George Whitefield approved black slavery and kept slaves himself. In 1748 Whitefield and others urged the trustees of Georgia to introduce slavery into the colony arguing that without slavery Georgia would not be prosperous.

I must confess that I was repeatedly tempted to divert into the realm of critical critique of some scholars, historical and political situations. Rather than the academic and intellectual peregrination in scholarship I have academically travelled away from the path of critique. I have therefore concentrated on Dis-empowerment and Engagement- Raising Consciousness which was the basic and fundamental philosophy of enslavement. The Europeans and British policy and programme in the transatlantic slave trade in Africans was to make all Africans permanently powerless. The enslavers, planters, merchants and churches parcelled-up dysfunctionalism with permanent paralysis and imposed it on the black-race. Dis-empowerment and powerlessness were pestiferous plots, ambition, programme and philosophy of Europeans and British against Africans Racially. The moral evil was bound up with the transatlantic (Black African) racial slave trade. The missionary movement and theology were inseparable. It is a major reiteration legacy politically, economically and psychologically affecting Africans and Diasporas alike today. Lastly, Black Empowerment is still an epistemological dream for the majority of Africans and Diasporas. Africans and Diasporas need to recapture the African slaves pertinacious and (katagma) catagmatic spirit and the ancestors will bridge the spirit of the cosmic energy. Building and Raising Consciousness socially, politically, educationally and theologically is deeply imperative and urgent for all of Africa and the Diasporas. Kebuka "Remembering The Middle Passage Through The Eyes of Our Ancestors."And Maafa. Great Destruction through 500 years of brutal racialised enslavement of the Black Race.

Dr. Robinson A. Milwood July 2010 RAM Theological Seminary

Acknowledgements

Dis-empowerment and Engagement- Raising Consciousness came out of a conversation I had with my wife on Africa's Infrastructure. My approach in this thesis is a radical ground-breaking and provocative approach critically articulated. Many insights and indications on the subject gave birth to great challenges. Pan-Africanism and the Diasporas are significant to a greater perspicuous application and contribution.

The study of the transatlantic (Black African) slave trade in Africans is a dynamic subject and the evolutionary attitude to modern black scholarship mixed with liberation theology and black theology is tremendously empowering. The reliance is no longer based simply on historical records, monographs and historical literatures. The shift has moved to the discovery of tremendous Slaves Narratives and scientific sources. Helen Thomas has delineated this fact sagaciously in her book on Romanticism and Slave Narratives Transatlantic Testimonies.2000. The major studies does include the importance of histographical literature. Greater attention and appreciation to the Transatlantic slave trade (Slavery) in Africans as the fundamental source of European and British economic foundations which Prof. James Walvin acknowledged in his book Black Ivory. Prof. Walvin's acknowledgement that transatlantic slave trade in African slavery was the economic foundation of Europe and Britain is a new understanding from the British school of thought.

Many white scholars tried to play down the dynamic importance of slavery and economic hegemony to Europe and Britain. Juxtaposed to this was the major churches involvement politically and theologically.

Dr. Eric Williams- Capitalism and Slavery is scholarship of eximious quality. Before or in recent years the propinquity between slavery and the economic foundation was not looked upon as of paramount importance. The reality is that historically the transatlantic (Black African) slave trade was the economic foundation stone of European countries and Britain. In other words, the transatlantic slave trade in Africans was an institution created for the dissipation of Africa but for the benefit of Europe and Britain. African free labour was central to the British Industrial Revolution, political and economical position in the world according to Dr. Eric Williams in his book Capitalism and Slavery. Slavery was the heart and engine of Europe, Britain and the USA. Its importance had been ignored for a very long time as the foundation stone because of moral, political, and theological reasons by governments and church leaders. In addition, it was blatant dis-respect, dis-regard for black people's contributions on the grounds of cultural racism.

Thanks to eximious scholars such as C.L.R James, Dr. Eric Williams, Dr. Richard Hart, Dr. David Beck Ryden, Dr. Verene Shepherd and Dr. Hilary Mac. Beckles. Prof. Seymour Drescher Abolition. A History of Slavery and Antislavery. Nicholas Draper The Price of Emancipation. Thavolia Glymph Out of the House of Bondage. Rebecca J. Scott Degrees of Freedom. Paul E. Lovejoy Identity in the Shadow of Slavery, Mwalimu Baruti, Kebuka. Remembering the Middle Passage Through the Eyes of Our Ancestors, Slavery edited by Stanley Engerman, Seymour Drescher and Robert Paquette, Transatlantic Slavery Against Human Dignity, edited by Anthony Tibbles., Black British History edited by

David Dabydeen, John Gilmore and Cecil Jones, for their appreciative and prodigious contributions in the study of the transatlantic slave trade in Africans.

I am academically indebted to these eximious giants of scholars for their academic contributions to the research and study of the transatlantic slave trade in Africans. Acknowledgement is due to the Jamaican-American scholar Prof. Anne C. Bailey for her book "African Voices of the Atlantic Slave Trade- Beyond the Silence and the Shame". Pan-Africanism and Regionalism The J. B. Danquah Memorial Lecture by Prof. S.K.B. Asante has been helpful with reservation as I was compelled to dismissed Dr. Asante explanation and expectation of Diasporas as only "financial" to Africa and his serious failure to see the important contributions of the Diasporas on Africa. Harriet Jacobs "Incidents in the Life of a Slave Girl" added to the powerful engagement of women in slavery. Phillis Wheatley C. L. R. James A history of Negro Revolt played an illuminating process in the writing of the thesis. Rev'd. John M. Turner M.A. discussed with me and provided for me a copy of John Wesley's critique on slavery.1774. Thoughts upon Slavery.

I have paid appreciative laudation to the slave leaders Rebellions and Insurrections by males and females slaves in their rightful quest for total manumission from slavery and their decisive contributions in the dictation and formulation of the time-table for Abolition and Emancipation. The Hayti revolution under the leadership of Toussaint L'Ouverture was the culmination of various slaves wars and rebellions. I find these consistently inspiring to the intellect and the confidence in making far reaching postulations with radical interpretations of the historical accounts.

Special thanks to my wife Priscilla and daughters, Chrystal and Miriam for their brilliant understanding and encouragement during the period of my indagation at Oxford. The countless dialogues we have had, all helped in the shaping of this thesis. To Blackwell Bookshop Oxford and Rhodes House Oxford for the supply of books and other relevant materials, many thanks. In my list of thanks and sodality, a stupendous thanks to a prodigious Black sister and extraordinary friend, Mrs. Claudette Igiehon M.A. B.Sc. for proof-reading the MS.

There is no other human race on earth with the African story and journey. The history and stories of the transatlantic (Black African) slave trade in Africans is powerful. The encapsulation of 500 years of brutal enslavement at the hands of European and British people who were purportedly described and defined as civilised and most arrogantly claimed to be Christians. They are politically, economically, theologically and morally responsible for the extermination through the transatlantic slave trade in Africans for the brutal deaths of 280.000.000 -300,000.000 Africans. It is not a simple story of slaves and enslavement. It is not a story of canty and sodality or Chimericalism. It is what I called a profligate system.' A system of racism and hatred. Re'd. Dr. James Ramsey called the slave trade- an institution. Ramsey was a medical doctor and an ordained minister and a missionary in Jamaica. Prof. Roger Anstey called the transatlantic slave trade 'a dynamic system'. Prof. Anstey was a Methodist Minister and Professor of Modern History at Kent University. Prof. James Walvin called the transatlantic slave trade' a moral repugnant system'. Prof. Walvin was Prof. of History at York University. Prof. David Byron Davis called the transatlantic slave trade compensation to the farmers, planters, enslavers and merchants 'Pragmatic Necessity.' Prof. Davis is Prof. of History at Yale University. Prof. David Beck Ryden called the transatlantic slave trade 'the retarded source of the advancement of Africa.' Prof. Ryden is associate professor of history at University of Houston. Dr. Anthony Brown called the transatlantic slave trade 'great political evil'. Edward Long called the transatlantic slave trade 'a national sin'. But the reiteration legacies and traumatic syndromes today is continuing the story of the African Race and Diasporas dis-empowerment, dysfunctionalism, paralysis and powerlessness. The historical legacies of the transatlantic slave trade in Africans was based on white racism and religious cultural Infralapsarianism theologically. One can use audacity or with temerity and state frankly that the transatlantic slave trade in Africans was the outlet and emission for European and British Racism. It was Racism bound up in economic rapacity, cultural superiority, theology, philosophy of religion, Evangelization and Christianization of Africans by the major churches mentioned above without any moral content and integrity. The churches perceived that there were no incongruity between enslavement of Africans and European and British Christianity.

Dr. Robinson A. Milwood. July 2010. RAM Theological Seminary London

Dedication

I dedicate this book to my wife Priscilla and our daughters Miriam and Chrystal for their ebullience and encouragement with my academic commitment.

Chapter 1
Technical Words and Terminologies Explained

This thesis on Dis-empowerment and Engagement, Raising-Consciousness is a radical ground-breaking thesis which it is hoped will instigate and encourage further systematic analysis and investigative study. I have consciously used what might be for some readers unfamiliar words and terminologies. These words and terminologies are necessary to evaluate and to define the different types of Traumatic Syndromes the slave had to go through and endured. These had sociologically and psychologically impacted on Africa and the Diasporas. The development of the traumatic syndromes were the slaves existential and empirical journey and situations. Enmeshed in the culture of brutality, humiliation, dehumanization and indignity beyond ordinary vocabulary. Random and persistent beating, breaking of bones, iron crooks secured about necks, smashing out of eyes, ear slitting and castration were very common. Unless these terminologies are used correctively, the process to understand, re-connect and experience psychologically, emotionally, spiritually and physically the slaves experiences, the reconnection envisaged in raising- consciousness will be very difficult.

There can be no meaningful psychological and spiritual re-connection with the transatlantic slave trade without a good understanding of these imperative words and terminologies. My daughter Chrystal insisted that I should make all the technical words and terminologies very clear. This I shall endeavour to do, without losing the verve and application of the words in human context, especially the black context of the transatlantic slave trade in Africans.

Villagization Traumatic Syndrome

Slaves lived in their demographical environment based on village life with relative comfort and the tenacity of the groups, tribes or clans communities. These communities comprised of chiefs, the elders and paramount chiefs. Customs were deeply ingrained, traditions linked to the gods of ancestors, tribal gods, tribal tires, kingship, religious customs, reverence for the tribal traditions. Traditional burial of the dead was a significant custom. In addition, funeral rights. Traditional family customs of marriage. Respect for the elders was deeply ingrained in the African culture. The division of Africa into 53 countries came about at the Berlin Conference in 1884-85. Domestic slavery was not brutal. There was no form of chattel slavery before the arrival of the Europeans and British. It is a myth that domestic slaves had no rights. Domestic slaves had rights. Even in Europe slaves had rights. Hugh Thomas made this point in his book on the Slave Trade.

Slavery in the villages was not like European and British cattle slavery. Domestic slavery was not a system or institution. Village slavery was not enforced uprooting of individuals or groups. Dr. Helen Thomas in her outstanding book on Romanticism and Slave Narratives defined Diaspora as "dispersal, fragmentation, displacement, enslavement and transportation experienced by African peoples and their descendants, experiences which unified such peoples at the same time as cutting them off from direct access to their past." Villagization was honourable. It was the Europeans, British and Americans who penetrated the villages with tricks, guns, whisky and rum. Europeans and British alike also encouraged wars between kingdoms, tribes and chiefs in order to capture the people for slavery. It was the racial culture of Europeans and British to divide and rule. The Europeans, British and Americans were brutal people with a rapscallion mentality and culture. It was a mindset enveloped in what they called Christianity. It was a cultural semantical Christianity vacuous of morality in contents and integrity.

Kidnapping of village people by Europeans, British and Americans was for economic reasons. The removal of men, women and children forcefully from their village community straight into the bondage of enforced enslavement physically, emotionally and psychologically was the beginning of the experience of traumatic syndrome. It was the beginning of the African displacement, psychological and sociological dislocation, demographical and anthropological tsunami. The brutal isolation from the village life and community. Enslavement was a foreign encounter and experience to the Africans. The painful journey across the terrain with chains and yokes for weeks to the most evil place created by Europeans and maintained by the British for nearly 150 years namely Cape Coast Castle or Elmina Castle in Ghana West Africa.

Dungeonization Traumatic Syndrome

The World Dictionary defined dungeon "as a dark underground room or cell to keep prisoners and to confine in a prison." The people who were captured were originally free people. Through kidnapping Europeans, British and Americans made Africans forcefully into prisoners for their economical enslavement, greed and racism. Europeans, British and

Americans enticed African chiefs into wars with guns in order that during fighting they would capture their citizens and placed them in the bondage of slavery. The slaves were confined in dungeons for up-to two months. The dungeons were beyond the imagination of any God fearing human being. The Europeans and British were heathens and pagans. They were demonically possessed with Racism and economic edacity.

There are over 53 Castles along the shores of Ghana, each with a dungeon. Cape Coast Castle is the largest with a dungeon capacity for 1000. The conditions of Elmina Castle is graphically described by William St Clair in his book "The Grand Slave Emporium" Cape Coast Castle and the British Slave Trade. The same book is under the title "The Door of No Return." My personal recollection of Cape Coast Castle is that the dungeon has only one entrance. Stretching one's hand forward, one cannot see one's fingers. On entering the dungeon the stench of death is over-powering. The stench of blood and faeces is overwhelming. The Missionaries, Merchants and Enslavers were (a) Pagans. (b) Heathens. (c) They had no known psychic- connections. (d) They had a psychic-distance. (e) The Catholic Church Communion Table above the dungeon is a clear demonstration and affirmation of the function of the Churches in the brutal enslavement of Africans in the Name of Almighty God, Christianity and a white Jesus Christ. The churches were the fore-runners of the Merchants, Royals, Enslavers and Traders. The churches were the major engines of the enslavement of Africans and the Institution of Slavery during the transatlantic slave trade in Africans.

The slaves who died in the dungeon would normally quickly because of the blood, faeces and other human waste started to decompose almost immediately. The unhealthy environment precipitated decomposing. The slaves were forced to live for up-to eight weeks and more in this diabolical and heinous condition because they were perceived to be black animals. The slaves were dehumanized and humiliated in the name of white civilization and Christianity. Dr. John Trapham who was the Worthy Park plantation doctor in Jamaica defined blacks "to the alleged fact, that they were an "animal people" Those slaves that rebelled were taken to another under-ground area and left there to suffer and die. It was (The Door of NO Return). The black slaves experienced horrendous traumatic syndromes. The dungeonization traumatic syndrome was the beginning of a life of hell. It was devastating. There are markings on the ground and on the walls in the dungeons made by dying slaves. In 2008 it was scientifically and archeologically confirmed that the ground of the dungeon at Elmina Castle was covered with 12ins of faeces built over the slave period. The faeces had formed solid as concrete. This was the creation of the dungeonization traumatic syndrome for African slaves. African people were enslaved fundamentally because of their racial origin. It was European and British capacity to hate, to be evil, to be callous, and to be immoral and extreme racist.

The Government of Ghana and the Diaspora should join forces and preserve Cape Coast Castle as the Mecca for all Africans and the Diasporas. I would urge all black people world-wide to make a conscious commitment before life ends to make a pilgrimage to Elmina Castle Ghana. It would be difficult for any black person to visit Cape Coast Castle with a sense of reconnection and psychic connection, emotional and spiritual connections not to feel a profound sense of transformation. But it is to be admitted by the author of this thesis that two Methodist ministers reported to the author that they had been to Cape Coast Castle and I personally found these two ministers to be Racist to the extreme. I found them to be evil to the extreme. I found them deeply irreligious. I have no difficulty in fully identifying them with the people who kidnapped and enslaved Africans in the dungeon at Cape Coast Castle. They have no moral content and no moral integrity. They are in the Methodist Church today preaching to Africans and African-Caribbean people like Rev'd. George Whitefield who had his own slaves and he encouraged slavery. In a nut-shell, they have no theological and sociological apologetic.

Infibulation Traumatic Syndrome

The World Dictionary defined Infibulation as to fasten or confine with or as if with a buckle. The slaves were chained together on the slave ships in the hull of the ships and on deck. Those slaves who died were still infibulated. That is that they were chained together in life and death. The imagination of the state of the Middle Passage is a truncation to the human spirit and heart. The infibulations of the slaves lasted for between two months to three months on the transatlantic crossing namely the Middle Passage. Many slaves died on board, others during exercise grumped over-board. Many saw the Atlantic Ocean and death better than enslavement. This was a third traumatic syndrome for the slaves. Their enjoyment of freedom in Africa has been transformed into hell with this kind of infibulations. At the Liverpool National Museums there is dramatization of Infibulation on slave ships.

Plantation Traumatic Syndrome

Slaves were auctioned to different plantations in the Caribbean, South America, Canada and the USA. They were treated like animals. The Africans were seen, looked upon and perceived to be animals. Even slaves doctors medically defined the slaves as animals. Slaves had to work long hours without proper nourishments. Slaves were deliberately kept in a state victual-less. Slaves were sexually abused openly on the plantations. Slaves men, women and children were sodomonized. The recent sexual abuse of adults and children in the Catholic Church is reminiscent of the transatlantic slave trade Middle Passage. The dungeons and plantations were their destination. Prof. James Walvin in his book (Black Ivory) graphically elaborated on this condition. Prof. Walvin said, that the slaves were whipped mercilessly. They were provided as (sexual) afters on Saturdays and Sundays by planters to be raped by other planters, friends, white workers and slave traders. Each plantation had a whipping post where slaves were whipped for small failures or refusal for sexual abuse. Slaves were hanged on tree limbs by one leg especially the women for the crows to eat them alive. Slaves had their limbs cut off. Slaves ears were also cut off and they were forced to eat their own ears. A regular punishment was for other slaves to defecate in the mouth of any defiant slave. Runaway slaves had blood-hound dogs set upon them and when caught according to Harriet Jacobs, had the flesh ripped from their bones in the presence of other slaves. Plantation slavery was brutal but it was a demonstration that the planters and enslavers were the representation of de-civilization. They were de-civilized pagans. Plantation slavery re-enforced the mental, physical and psychological states of traumatic syndromes for the slaves. Slaves had the sole of the feet cut off for punishment. White slave-holding women deliberately whipped their husbands slaves openly before an audience in order to demonstrate that they had equal power to the men.

Dr. Vincent Harding in his book "There is a River- The Black Struggle for Freedom in America told two lived stories which are significant here. David Walker claimed to have watched the degradation of two men: (1) a son who was forced to strip his mother naked and whip her until she died. (2) And a black husband forced to lash his pregnant wife until she aborted her child. Heterogeneity is here replaced with the forced imposition of Black hatred.

Barracoonization Traumatic Syndrome

Each plantation had its own barracoon. The barracoon was built by the slaves themselves. The World Dictionary definition is academically jejune. The best lived account of the barracoon environment, is that in Caribbean Slavery in the Atlantic World A Student Reader under the chapter title "The Autobiography of a Runaway Slave." Esteban Montejo as eye witness and personal testimony." All the slaves lived in barracoons. These dwelling places no longer exist, so one cannot see them. But I saw them and I never thought well of them. The masters, of course, said they were as clean as new pens. The slaves disliked living under those conditions: being locked up stifled them. The barracoons were large, though some plantations had smaller ones; it depended on the number of slaves in the settlement. Around two hundred slaves of all colours lived in the Florde Sagua barracoon. This was laid out in rows; two rows facing each other with a door in the middle and a massive padlock to shut the slaves in at night. There were barracoons of wood and barracoons of masonry with tiled roofs. Both types had mud floors and were as dirty as hell. And there was no modern ventilation there.' Just a hole in the wall or a small barred window. The result was that the place swarmed with fleas and ticks, which made the inmates ill with infections and evil spells, for those ticks were witches. The only way to get rid of them was with hot wax, and sometimes even that did not work. The masters wanted the barracoons to look clean outside, so they were whitewashed. The job was given to the Negroes themselves. As the rooms were so small the slaves relieved themselves in a so-called toilet standing in one corner of the barracoon. Everyone used it. And to wipe your arse afterwards you had to pick leaves and maize husks."

Pregnant women were kept in the plantation infirmary near the barracoon, a big wooden hut where they took the pregnant women. You were born there and stayed there till you were six or seven, when you went to live in the barracoons and began work like the rest.

"I saw many horrors in the way of punishment under slavery. That was why I didn't like the life. The stocks which were in the boiler-house, were the cruellest. Some were for standing and others for lying down. They were made of thick planks with holes for the head, hands and feet. They would keep slaves fastened up like this for two or three months for trivial offence. They whipped the pregnant women too, but lying face down with a hollow in the ground for their bellies. They whipped them hard, but took good care not to damage the babies because they wanted as many of those as possible. The most common punishment was flogging; this was given with a rawhide lash which made weal's on the skin. They also had whips made of the fibres of some jungle plant which stung like the devil and flayed the skin off in strips. I saw many handsome big Negroes with raw backs. Afterwards the cut were covered with compresses of tobacco leaves, urine and salt."

Another feature of barracoon life was that it was for breeding. The masters picked the fittest young men and women and placed them in small rooms in the barracoons for breeding purposes. They were animals for breeding to keep the supply of slaves. Esteban Montejo included in his dramatic eye witnessed story the function of the Catholic church. The priests introduced religion to the slaves in the barracoon condition but says Montejo the priests would not enter the slaves quarters.

It is with justification for the author to point out forcefully that the slaves suffered physical punishments, psychological, emotional and spiritual punishments. The causes of the various types of traumatic syndromes are self-evident. This does, as I have expressed in other writings, called into question the existence of an omnipotent God. Does God Exist? No wonder white philosophers and white theologians past and present never include in their theological and philosophical curriculum on Suffering and Evil, the Transatlantic (Black African) Slave trade. The transatlantic slave trade was morally repugnant. It was a pestiferous crime against a Morally good God and humanity according to Dr. David Beck Ryden. Black people have all rights to question radically every aspect of white Theology and Philosophy. These are based on extreme-racism Cultural Religion and Racism. It is imperative and urgent for black ministers and theologians to interpret God, Christianity and Jesus Christ from the historical context of the oppressions, exploitations, de-humanizations and humiliations of Africans during the transatlantic slave trade. Especially in the context of the enslavement racially of Africans as consistent with white Christianity, Religion, God and a white Jesus Christ.

Infaticidezation Traumatic Syndrome

The World Dictionary defined infaticidezation as a person who kills a baby. Slave mothers, destroyed their child / children sometimes before birth despite the degree of punishment. Others killed their child at birth, rather than to allow the child to grow up on the plantation into slavery at the age of six or seven years. Mothers suffered tremendous traumatic syndromes from infanticide. The brutality and heinous-ness is in permeation and is difficult to curtail during the period of slavery.

Deracination Traumatic Syndrome

According to the World Dictionary Deracination is to tear up by the roots. Uprootment was not normal for Africans. Exterminate and deracinate is to be uprooted from one's native or natural geographical locality. The dissipation of African Cultures, Religious Beliefs, Customs and Traditions was the purpose of the transatlantic Slave

Trade in the Africans. Deracination is likened to villagization traumatic syndrome. It was the forceful brutal uprooting of Africans from their communities into bondage and full slavery. Elephants experienced the impact of drastic post-traumatic syndrome through uprooting and it is well attested scientifically that such uprooting has seriously impacted on Elephants behaviour. The slaves who jumped overboard into the Atlantic Ocean rather than endure slavery, is a good illustration. Some slaves poisoned themselves. Uprooting was a deep cause for tremendous traumatic syndromes among the surviving slaves. The impacts cannot be overstated. Slavery was hell. The churches and missionaries were more than audacious to have used evangelization and Christianization in the enslavement of Africans. According to Dr. Richard Hart in his book (Slaves Who Abolished Slavery) The enslavers objected to the missionaries introducing Christianity to their slaves. The enslavers claimed that European and British Christianity was for Europeans and British only. It was at this point that the (brain-washing) kicks in effectively, of which the Methodist was the main leaders.

Animalization Traumatic Syndrome

European and British Racism claimed that Africans were sub-human. That they were not fully human. This was the regular contention of philosophers, theologians, scientists, anthropologist and historians. This concept was moulded into the culture of Europe and Britain. Africans were synonymous with animals. They were treated as such. Africans were looked upon as beast of burden. They had no soul and no feelings. The reduction of Africans to this beastly level radically affected their humanity, characteristics and dignity. The synthesization of the above mentioned traumatic syndromes does highlight for us the reiteration legacies of traumatic syndromes among the Africans Diasporas. Africans were kept intellectually ignorant in order to reinforced the white concept that Africans were animals. Dr. David Beck Ryden said that "slaves were forced to live in a Hobbesian land, were supposed to be lacking in the capacity to recognize moral choices or to reach their full potential."

Dehumanization Traumatic Syndrome

There is concomitant synthesis with animalization generally. All human characteristics and attributes were denied the Africans by the enslavers and missionaries. The power of thinking and communication was denied the slaves. Slaves were not allowed to learn to read or write. The philosophy was to keep the slaves in a complete state of ignorance and powerlessness. Thus making them like animals. They were conditioned to think and to accept that they had animal qualities for the justification of enslavement as Africans. Demographically the slaves suffered tremendous (demographical-psychological-geographical traumatic syndromes). The slaves languages and dialectics were banned and commixed in order to create confusion and the imposition of the slave master's language.

Stultification Traumatic Syndrome

The merchants and enslavers had a deep form of European and British Racism in the inculcation of the slaves by the churches, enslavers, merchants and slave traders who believed that Africans only worth was to be slaves. (That God created Africans to be slaves) Many Missionaries, theologians, philosophers and scientists believed that Africans were biologically inferior to whites. The Methodist Church doctrinally and theologically claimed that Africans were inherently inferior to whites. That Africans were programmed and biologically ordained to work hard and be slaves. Paradoxically, the major denominations tasks was this form of inculcation which was a doctrine of stultification. Stultification is not only linked to the transatlantic slave trade and plantation slavery.

The slaves had no rights; they were not entitled to know or experienced freedom. The missionaries were taught not to use words such as Freedom, love, peace, forgiveness, justice, liberty, manumission and equality to the slaves. The Methodist Missionary minister The Rev'd. John Smith was given unequivocal instructions not to allow to flow out of his mouth Words such as, freedom, justice, peace, equality and reconciliation. For the enslavers and churches the slaves had no emotional feelings. They were beast of burden. The inculcation of stultification runs deep educationally, psychologically, culturally and emotionally with Africans and African -Caribbean people, both adults and young people. Stultification is a damaging function of the reiteration legacies today common among African-descendants in Britain.

Stultification runs deep in the psyche of Africans and African-Caribbean descendants. The educational systems today generates a sense of stultification among young Black people. It is a traumatic syndrome which is part of the re-iteration legacies of historical slavery. Basically to make a person or community dysfunctional within a community of paralysed people because of oppression. It is furthermore the evidence of not having any respect for the individual or community. It is a means of robbing the person or community of their dignity. The South African Apartheid System demonstrated the full purpose of stultification of the indigenous Africans. Demographically Africans are stultified people, they are a people inundated with paralysis, economically, sociologically, technologically and psychologically. The World Dictionary's definition is that it is to make someone worthless and useless, weak, or futile. To stultify a person's efforts or incentive. A program of reform stultified by public indifference It is to make a person or community of people to have vacant-esteem. Along-side stultification is psychological powerlessness. The philosophy behind the (Black African) transatlantic slave trade was one of stultiloquence. (To make foolish, Silly, Senseless), (stultiloquentia- stultiloquus), speaking foolishly. It was a developed and dynamic system by Europeans and British alike with their deep cultural Racism. Many African Diasporas are in the main still suffering from endemic sociological and psychological Stultification Traumatic Syndrome which is a Post Traumatic Slave Syndrome.

Routinization Traumatic Syndrome

The World Dictionary explains routinization as to cause to become a routine, make habitual. To routinize a process or operation, to routinize religion. A better explanation is the biblical story of the African people in slavery in Egypt. Moses was confronted by a fragmented group of people who were physically and psychologically dominated by the routinization of slavery for over 400 years. Their routinization became a psychological routinization in that all they knew mentally was slavery. Let's take the paradigm one stage further. A race-horse that is trained for running, knows nothing else but running.

Slave children born on the plantation barracoons and auctioned to plantations at the age of 3years- grew up on the plantations- worked, lived and discarded by old age or over-worked by routinization. The physical, spiritual and psychological routinization traumatic syndrome was a tremendous problem especially physically for the slaves.

It is historically correct to point out that the system of routinization was the basic function of plantation slavery. Routinization was the system or process to obtained the maximum volume of work and labour out of each slave. For the enslaves who were enslaved there were no tomorrow for liberation. The economic pull for the European and British economies demands for their economies the driving force of slavery. It is what Prof. Roger Anstey called "the dynamic system." It was 500 years of brutal and hostile routinization of the slaves lives, created by a lasting routinization traumatic syndrome. It became a post traumatic syndrome. Slaves had no freedom, no rights, no dignity; they were completely and comprehensively stultified mentally. They were brain-washed to believed that heaven was their reward for their brutal enslavement, confirmed by a religion and theology of Infralapsarianism. This was a vapid cultural claim theologically. The Methodist Church claimed that Africans were inherently inferior to white people. The Methodist Church claimed this position with theological justification. There is a significant difference theologically even with the Anglican Church which had slaves plantations and their Bishops and Archbishops had slaves. The prodigious Rev'd. Dr. James Ramsey who started the abolition debate he too had slaves. The fundamental difference between the Methodists and the Anglicans was that "the Anglican Church called for an International Conference to debate the theological justification for slavery."

Slaves were forcefully conditioned brutally and heartlessly to the identical living conditions of a systematic routinization from birth to death. The ultimate degree of routinization traumatic syndrome was the endless station of being a slave from birth to death. Liberty and equality was denied all African slaves. Slavery was the slaves karma. Penologically the slaves were trapped in the penology of routinization physically and psychologically. The pulverization of the slaves by the force of routinization is a physical and psychological reiteration traumatic syndrome legacy that Africans and Diasporas are facing today in different situations and conditions globally.

Pummelization Traumatic Syndrome

The World Dictionary defines pummel-meled-melling, melled to strike or beat with the fists. The slaves were conditioned to physical punishments in the forms of whipping, especially at the whipping post. They were conditioned by fear. They were conditioned to brutality with the emission of hatred and racism. A sense of superiority and the might of economical power by forceful enslavement and the deduction of free African labour for 500 years.

The slaves were beaten physically, spiritually and psychologically into complete submission that slavery became for them their alpha and omega. In this dramatic system of oppression and exploitation the churches were the driving- force and at the centre of this barbaric act of slavery.

Infralapsarianism Traumatic Syndrome

The World Dictionary definition needs some form of praxeology (praxiology) to fully understand the Theology of Infralapsarianism that was practiced by the churches. I deliberately declined using the prefix (Christian) before churches. The composition of people who were enmeshed in the transatlantic (Black African) slave trade were as I have explained else-where in this academic in-da-ga-tion especially that the churches were pagans and heathens. Just a simple reminder, namely, that the Anglican Church through the Bishops and Archbishops had their own slaves and plantations. The Anglican Church called for an International indaba to decide on the theological justification of the enslavement of Africans.

Infralapsarianism (Infralapsarian) was a Theology developed by the churches. It was a doctrine that God decreed the division of mankind into the elect and the damned after the Fall and not from Eternity. The missionaries believed in the doctrine of infralapsarianism of Africans racially. They classified Africans as non-beings. They believed that Africans were animals. That they were creatures without a soul. Africans were in their eyes totally uncivilized. They promoted the theology that God made Africans to be slaves for the whites. The churches claimed that their white Christianity was consistent with Slavery. In addition they saw no incongruity between enslaving Africans and their white cultural semantical Christianity.

Historically, religion, science, theology, doctrines, philosophy, engineering, medicine and embalmment began in Africa. All theological concepts began in Africa. The Monotheistic belief is an African concept. African missionaries carried these prodigious African traditions to Europe. Europeans acculturated the African Christianity and then turned it into a white culture and system, and then used it in the scheme of enslavement of Africans in the name of Almighty God and Christianity and a white Jesus.

Prof. Runoko Rashidi an African American in his book "The Global African Community" Travel Notes. He has shown the powerful presence of Africans throughout Europe and Britain. It is a significant reminder that Britain had always been a pagan nation. The Dark Ages.

Myalism was an African Religion which came into confrontation with the Moravian church during the transatlantic slave trade in the 18th century. The confrontation lasted for one hundred years in the US and one hundred years in Jamaica. Basically, Africans were deeply religious people. They were contiguous to the Ancestorial Gods, Spirits and Ancestors. They had a remarkable knowledge and awareness of

Cosmology. The world was for Africans harmonious with all creatures. God was to be experienced through the manifestations of nature and the higher planets.

The Missionaries and enslavers went to Africa with a European and British Semantical Christianity as instructed by Thomas Buxton that all the missionaries had to give to Africa regardless of the multitude of sins was "religious instructions." Therefore, the missionaries repudiated and invalidated every form of African religious beliefs and practices. They then imposed their Racism in the form of European and British Christianity for the immoral enslavement of Africans.

Prof. Diarmaid MacCulloch in his major volume entitled "A History of Christianity" reminds us "that the link between blackness and slavery reached the Christian West late, and it was ironically via Judaism. Just when the Portuguese were beginning to take their share of the African slave trade, in the late fifteenth century, a celebrated Portuguese Jewish philosopher, Isaac Ben Abravanel, suggested that Canaan's descendants were black, while those of his uncles were white, and so all black people were liable to be enslaved. Gen.9 gives no support to this belief and Abravanel's innovative exercise in biblical hermeneutics proved extremely convenient for the same Iberian Christians who persecuted his own people, and later for Christian slavers everywhere." Prof. MacCulloch goes on to say that Genesis 4.1-16: "according to this Syriac take on the biblical text, black people actually descended from Cain because when God had punished Cain for killing his brother Abel, the "mark" he gave the murderer was to blacken his skin. It was reasonable to suppose that this applied to all Cain's descendants. Neither biblical approach was calculated to raise the status of people defined as black. It took original minds to kick against the authority of sacred scripture.

What was needed was a prior conviction in one's conscience of the wrongness of slavery."

I laudate Dr. MacCulloch with appreciative hesitation because the missionaries and medical doctors of the transatlantic (Black African) slave trade saw no moral or theological incongruity between their Christianity and Slavery. Their theology of Infralapsarianism. This was a spiritual, psychological and theological traumatic experience for the slaves. The inculcation was horrendous. It stretched the inner psyche of the slaves. It had impacted profoundly on the slaves.

Humiliation Traumatic Syndrome

All slaves were treated with the same brush of racism and superiority. Oppression, exploitation and brutal enslavement. The slaves were legally defined as chattels. The legal definition was reinforced theologically by the enslavers and missionaries. Paradoxically, the enslavers labelled themselves Christians. Rev. Dr. James Ramsey was an Anglican minister of religion and he was at the same-time a medical doctor. He too saw no incongruity between being a medical doctor and a minister of religion in the West Indies.

In the various dungeons throughout West Africa and Nigeria, the slaves were packed in the same dungeons. The slave ships were no different. Male and Female slaves shared imbrications and infibulations alike. The random demand for sex by the slave masters. Slaves were deliberately humiliated because they were chattels. Their dignity was stripped. They were reduced to beast of burden. They were fully stultified at all levels. They had no soul and no feelings. God made them that way to be slaves. Children were seen as little pigs. Little black monkeys. Little pet-dogs. All these treatments conditioned the slaves to developed the humiliation traumatic syndrome.

Historical Traumatic Syndrome

Also known as Historic Stress Syndrome it was first developed by Dr. NA'IM Akbar in his book "Breaking The Chains of Psychological Slavery." He is a prodigious African American Psychologist. Followed contiguously to Dr. Akbar is Dr. Joy Leary in her ground-breaking book "Post Traumatic Slave Syndrome." She too is an African American woman. Further reading is possible from these two USA Black scholars.

Excortication Traumatic Syndrome

The World Dictionary defined Excortication as the act of stripping off or peeling the bark, rind or coating from. The slaves were literally stripped of all human characteristics. They were racially scientifically, legally and theologically defined as chattels. The transatlantic slave trade in Africans was based on chattel slavery. The slaves were legally defined as properties. Beast of burden without a soul. That God created Africans to be slaves for Europeans and the British. That God had determined Africans to be slaves because of their colour. Some historians and theologians such as Prof. Roger Anstey (British Methodist Minister and historian) claimed that the brutal enslavement of Africans was part of God's Salvation History. The slaves were branded with hot iron like cows and mules. Slaves were sexually abused publicly. Men, women and children were sodomized frequently. Men were not allowed to wear clothes. In the Barracoons, slaves were placed to breed like animals to populate the masters plantations. Slaves were brutally killed for insurance claims. Slaves had no rights. Slaves were stultified mentally, psychologically and physically. Slaves had no names but only a number. Slaves were punished by allowing other slaves to practice defecation in the mouth of run-away slaves or rebellious slaves. Slaves were told that they were animals and they were treated as such. Slaves were subjected to constant oppression. Slaves were over-worked for economical profits. Men had no right over slave women. The slave masters had all rights. Slave women, young women were perpetually raped and they were provided for slave masters friends and colleagues to have as their afters on Saturdays and Sundays after dinner. Slave women were given and hired out to other plantations for perpetual rape by several men. Slaves were whipped at the whipping post to death. Slave women were hanged on tree limbs alive to be eaten alive by the crows for refusing the sexual advances of the slave masters and enslavers. Slaves were reduced to powerlessness and improvidence. Slaves were deliberately kept in total ignorance in order for enslavement and control of their lives. Slaves were traumatized spiritually and psychologically. Slaves were forcefully given the slave masters names. Slaves were not allowed to carry or have anything characterising the African customs and traditions. Their religions or halidoms. At the end of slavery the slaves were left totally illiterate, destitute, [powerless and backward.) Slaves were imprisoned in dungeons for long period of time before transporting across the Middle Passage. Slaves were packed like sardines in the hull of ships. These conditions were the total excortication of Africans humanity and dignity. The excortication of slaves from the category of human to dehumanization was with the involvement and approval of the European and British Churches with a doctrine of Racism and a theology of Infralapsarianism. The churches claimed that they had theological justification. (The Methodist Church affirmed this doctrine) The Anglican Church audaciously called for an International Conference to decide/discuss the theological justification for slavery. In other words, the churches wanted to doctrinally imposed their theological and historical concept of Infralapsarianism. Slaves were hanged or gibbeted alive. The excortication of the slaves was the full emission of European and British Racism enmeshed in their religion. They claimed moral, racial and cultural authority over the slaves. It was their white semantical cultural religious beliefs in action.

Propinquity (propinquus) **Traumatic Syndrome**

According to The World Book Dictionary Propinquity means (nearness in place, especially personal nearness. 2. Nearness of blood; kingship). Through my academic forensic hermeneutic research techniques and hermeneutic methodology I have discovered that the slaves suffered this particular severe traumatic stress syndrome. Historically, sociologically, culturally, religiously and psychologically Africans has been a very gregarious people. Separation came about by the introduction of the European and British cultures during the transatlantic slave trade. The dramatic removal of the people from their families, environment, customs and traditions.

In the religious traditions of Africans there are abundance of practices relating to the spirit of the ancestors and the dead. It is spiritually and psychologically very deep in their psyche and religious cultures. The bond between tribes and groups, mothers and fathers, brothers and sisters. In addition the slave trade shared experience cemented the African-Americans propinquity as genealogically Africans. The rapid and sudden encounter of separation from blood-relatives by the enforcement of slavery was a tremendous trauma in itself for the slaves being carried across the Atlantic and unto the brutal plantations to work like beast of burden in the heat of the sun for the glorification and pleasures of European and the British economic well being. Slavery was the under-pinning of the British economic foundation.

The lack of propinquity replaced by the force and impact of heterogeneity with the demographical changes and conditions further impacted on the spirit and psyche of the slaves. The sense of disconnection from the family, tribes or groups. From religion and customs with the power of traditions added to the trauma of the slaves. Genealogy is the para-genesis that keeps groups of people together and divisions will dislocate that vital and significant link. The African Diasporas seem to have lost that significant link with the passage of time and the deliberate inculcation of disunity by the missionaries on the minds of the slaves. Not only disunity and hatefulness of each other, but psychologically mistrust, dis- harmony and dis-respect. Here lies the reiteration legacy among Africans and the Diasporas.

Vilification Traumatic Syndrome

The World Dictionary definition of the word vilification is to speak evil of someone, to revile someone, to act with evil intension, to revile or to slander, to act with profligation, in a wicked way, to make morally vile.

A good student of the Dictionary will include the word vilipend which is to have very little value or consequence. It is to treat contemptuously. The period of the transatlantic slave trade lasted for 500 years of this type of treatment daily without hope or light for an end. European and British Racism in the form of racial slavery pulverised the Black race into insignificance psychologically, sociologically and theologically.

Degradation/Aggradations

Again the World Dictionary definition is to degrade. Make condition to deteriorate. The churches degraded Black people to the level of animals. Black people the churches claimed had no soul. Black people they said, were made by God to be slaves. African women were sexed openly on the plantations and in the streets like dogs, pigs, goats and cows. The women were totally dominated by the slave masters. They were chattels. Properties legally defined.

I am indebted to Dr. Akbar and Dr. Leary for their inspirations and incisive postulations of Post-traumatic slave syndrome and historical traumatic syndrome. Because of their contributions I have academically with serious indagation (research) come to the conviction and conclusion that the slaves had these traumatic syndromes impacted on them perpetually. Audaciously and academically I must say forcefully that the reiteration legacies of the transatlantic slave trade traumatic syndromes are very common among African-descendants. Much more work needs to be done on these traumatic syndromes. I have left out deliberately 1) Demographical Psychological Randomization traumatic syndrome and 2) Suboptimization traumatic syndromes, because I have dealt with these in my 2009 publication on the Psychological Combination of Christianity and Slavery. European and British endemic Racism is immedicable cultural disease. It is like their endemic culture of mendacity. The brutal enslavement of Africans was a very impervious pestiferous institution based on greed, economic exploitation and oppression of the African race through racial slavery, in the name of Almighty God, White Christianity and a White blue-eyed Jesus Christ.

The transatlantic (Black African) slave trade was the African tsunami. It was the African Holocaust. It was the African Genocide of 280.000.000-300.000.000 African men and women. (Two hundred and eighty million) Africans. (Three hundred million) This cannot be forgotten. Every attempt has been made for the 500 years and beyond of brutal enslavement of Africans to be forgotten by Africans and African-descendants. White scholars have perpetuated this deceptive scheme.

The traumatic syndromes discussed and defined above are effective dis-empowerment of the African race. It was a systematic programme. Slavery was a dynamic system and institution. No philosophical or theological ratiocination can influence historically the realities documented, lived and suffered by the African slaves. It is right to affirmatively confess that it is only the Black race which has the aggregate power to make the categorical statement, that Europe and Britain has no rectitudinous grounds "morally" "theologically." They have no solid ethical standing when the heinous and horrendous transatlantic slave trade is examined thoroughly by Black historians and Black liberation theologians. The humanitarian character, pictures and interpretations made by countless white scholars has been dissipated by the late Dr. Eric Williams in his book "British Historians and the West Indies. The intellectual gravity of Dr. Williams argument demands full attention from other scholars and students.

Middle-Passage Traumatic Syndrome (Kebuka)

The Liverpool National Museum or International Slavery Museum in Liverpool have an impressive simulation of the Middle Passage. Psychologically it is only a dramatization – simulation. Yet it has great impact that can instigate some limited measure of connection. Real connection comes from dynamic histographic information variously articulated. Professor James Walvin in his book "Black Ivory" Slavery in the British Empire under Part 11: Traumas- (3) Crossing the Atlantic has not grasped graphically the heinousness of the Middle-Passage. The barbarity of the Middle Passage experience. Dr. James Walvin failure is purely cultural and not personal.

Prof. Herbert S. Klein in his book "The Atlantic Slave Trade" relied only on the histographic literature rather than reliance on the psychological, emotional, spiritual and connected-consciousness. The genealogical and geographical connection are vitally important to Dr. Mwalimu K. Bomani Baruti thesis which he has confirmed for us in "Kebuka." (Remembering the Middle Passage Through the Eyes of our Ancestors) Dr. Baruti says, "See yourself, as you walk across the sand toward your floating destination, pretending to fall down so that you can scoop up a handful of dirt to hide in your mouth so that you can take your home with you." This is the noblest and highest level of human psychological, spiritual and geographical tangible connection. He continued, "As you travelled to the waiting (aliens ships) you remember names like the Egalite, Othello, Charming, Sally, Victorieux, Subordinateur, Reformation, Brotherhood, Liberty, Africa, Enterprise, Perseverance, Creole, Hare, Wolf, Sirene, John the Baptist, and so many added named after their mothers, fathers, sons, daughters, royalty, families, mythological figures, and country's favourite patron saints and deities including the Bomb Jesus." To these names I would personally add, St. Paul, St. Mathew, St. Luke and St. Mark. The Duke of Argle. Rev. John Newton's ship who was an evangelical minister of the Anglican church. Queen Elizabeth the 1 ship she gave to John Hawkins to loot Africa was (Jesus) for clarity.

"Stripped entirely naked, the slaves were packed into the stinking holes of the ships so close together that they were forced to sleep on their sides. With manacles on both their hands and feet, the slaves were then linked together by a continuous chain bolted to the floor."

"Most would spend the entirety of what was often a two or three-month journey in this position. A few depending on the mind or mood of the captain, would see the deck and daylight at mealtime or during other specified periods such as the torturously cruel exercise period when the slaves were made to dance in their heavy, cutting shackles."

"There was no turning over, no moving to rest one shoulder while the other began its painful journey into numbness. There was no turning around because the space was not available to stretch and the ceilings were too low. Feet in face, arm twisted and locked down, chains and metal cuffs shackling the twists and ankles of one brother to another, pores clogged, under conditions of intense heat, with no space for sweat to flow freely or air to enter because skin was pressed up so tightly against skin, urine, faeces and other bodily wastes poured onto each other and squeezed out between whatever paths they created between pressed skin. This was our ancestors' state for the months they were confined in this spoon position in these wretched places."

"Imagine lying in filth, disease, spittle, vomit, puss, slime, unidentifiable excretions from bedsores, fleas, ringworms and lice, yes, lice because they were so numerous on the crewmembers, and we had become so soiled that they had something to latch on to. Imagine worms, maggots in bodily waste, maggots thriving in the bedsores on your back, arms, legs and head, the whip's welts and the wounds cut and kept open by the metal cuffs locked to our wrists, ankles and sometimes necks (wounds) that salt water was often poured into to increase your pain under the lie of washing your skin."

"Imagine sweat, tears, human and rat faeces, blood, aborted fetuses, broken water, dead babies (yes, many captured women were pregnant when captured and many more were impregnated through their rape by sadistic aliens during the coffle marches and in the dungeons), afterbirth, screaming, moaning, numbing pain, living bodies not moving for days."

(Kebuka) Remembering The Middle Passage Through The Eyes Of Our Ancestors Mwalimu K. Bomani Baruti- describing the physical and psychic conditions of the slaves " What would it feel like to listen to yurugu's laughter as you remain unable to fend off psychic wave after psychic wave of your wife's and daughter's and sister's and mother's screaming? What would it feel like to watch a gang of European males beat your mother into semi-consciousness and then drag her body off away to what you know will be her repeated rape by every lusting, godless European in the vicinity?

Imagine them not being 'kind' enough to drag her out of sight to practice their sadism. Feel the rage of being forced to watch the desecration of the woman who brought you here, who fed you of her own body, who loved you every little bruise to health, your first teacher and final advisor. Imagine having witness your mother cry and scream in horror and pain as she is sexually tormented in the most sadistic ways the European mind could imagine over and over again right before your eyes.

"Imagine our queens being returned to their shackles in blood and tears, ashamed, enraged, lost, unable to look up. Think about how your beautiful, strong, soft, nurturing wife was reduced to a bloodied, bruised, naked, cowering shadow uncontrollably shaking beside a tree, jumping in blind flight every time a shadow moves or there is a noise in her vicinity, away from your protection, alone and afraid of when it will again be her turn to be viciously ravaged by those inhuman creatures."

As the pain forces you to suppress those unbearable images of your wife, watch as your mind continues to torture you with scenes of your nine-year-old daughter, numb with fear from her violation. Look into her eyes, terrified, horrified, pleading, consuming your every waking and sleeping moment. Remember her nakedness exposed you to her profuse bleeding, from her anus and vagina, from lacerations and gashes all about her body, physically, spiritually and psychologically wounded from being raped so many times and by so many each time that you knew she would never recover, lying motionless, mortified, her life force slowly but surely ebbing away into an abyss of irresolvable chaos." My conclusion on the dynamic description of the Middle Passage by Dr. Mwalimu K. Bomani Baruti in his book (Kebuka) Is that it is reasonable to postulate that the majority of the Black Race are without psychological equilibrium because of the impact of the heinous Middle Passage experience.'

Olaudah Equiano looking back thirty years, he had not forgotten the stink, said, "The smell was overpowering" "I was soon put down under decks, and there I received such a salutation in my nostrils as I had never experienced in my life; so that with the loathsomeness of the stench and crying together, I became so sick and low that I was not able to eat, nor had I the least desire to taste anything."

Equiano wrote his Narrative authentically from personal experience. In his campaign for abolition in England he was despised by the Methodist church as a member. He had various animadversions thrown at him, even the allegation that he was not an African from Nigeria, but rather a West Indian from Barbados.

The traumatic syndromes the slaves suffered in the Middle Passage was the fundamental formulation and basis for the developing traumatic syndromes. On this point we are told by Dr. Baruti again, 'Imagine clerics being brought on these voyages to watch over us. These are the same men of God who softened our minds with lies of a white god and a white salvation before their armies brought the rifle and cannon. Remember that these religious “fathers”, “rabbis” and other assorted “priests” “pastors” and “ministers” were as great, or even greater, enslavers as those who claimed no “calling” other than enslaver. Imagine these heathens praying for your soul.”

I am forced by the graphic gravity of these quotations to point out that it is unbelievable that white British scholars especially historians who have made the claim, that the transatlantic slave trade was a phenomena could have done any meaningful forensic hermeneutic indagation. These white scholars relied mainly on historical literatures and figures with chronologies. Many missionaries, slave-traders, merchants and enslavers claimed that slavery was good for Africans. Some claimed that the slaves were happy in slavery. How can 500 years of brutal, immoral enslavement of Africans by the churches, Methodist, Dutch Reformed, Anglican, Baptist, United Reformed, Moravian, Quakers Catholic and others hold on to this groundless claim? In addition, over 280,000.000 – 300.000.000 Africans died in the “Middle Passage” and Plantations exploitations. Slavery was racial. It was a combination of distance-psychic and extreme Racism by Europeans and British semantical-cultural Christianity. Added to this, the Jewish people hold on to the Jewish holocaust and the death of 6,000.000 Jews as the worst crime against humanity. Here the reiteration has moral and theological justification that the murder of 300,000.000 Africans was a crime against Almighty God and humanity. In addition the Jews had been paid handsomely and they continue to have annually billions of dollars from America. The Jews consistently delineate dis-respect for the UN and International Laws. While Africa has never received a mention of Reparation from Europe, Britain and the US.

Spiritualization Traumatic Syndrome

Throughout history Africans or the Black Race has always been deeply religious. Religious beliefs played a major part in the lives, communities, families, traditions and customs of all African people. The spiritual side of Africans played a powerful and meaningful function during the transatlantic slave trade period for the African slaves.

The custom of mourning for the dead or a loss member of the family or tribe. Religious rights over the deceased prior to the funeral service or at the time of the committal of the body. The dressing of the dead and libation. The festive side of the funeral service. In order not to allow the slaves to continue their religious funeral customs, the slave masters made sure that the body, bodies would be seriously mutilated thereby destroying the link between the living and the dead.

Africa was to be obliterated from the memory of the slaves. They were to receive a new religious orientation. It is indeed pretty obvious why the Moravian Church and community fought relentlessly with those traditions of African Myalism and Religious customs. The spiritual disconnection of the slaves was a gigantic challenge to the slave masters, the missionaries and theologians. Black Religion actually began during the slave trade period. Finally, with the examination of the various traumatic syndromes above with procacious steadfastness I believe that most of the Black race are without psychological equilibrium because the major engine of the transatlantic slave trade was the rapid spread of Christianity. Christianity according to Thomas Buxton was based on oppression. It was Racism enmeshed in white Christianity and culture. It was based on exploitation. It was a Christianity based on sodomization. It was a Christianity based on the religious and theological justification of racial superiority for the enslavement of the Black race.

Chapter 2
My Settled Intension

The dis-empowerment of Africans through the brutal, hateful, racialised and barbaric cruelty of African enslavement by Europeans and British with the rapid spread of semantical- cultural Christianity has created for African-descendants what appears to be a sempiternal trauma. I shall be examining a number of traumatic syndromes which are not listed by Dr. Joy Leary and Dr. Akbar in their scholarly books. Dr. Joy Leary. Post Traumatic Slave Syndrome and Dr. NA 'IM Akbar, Breaking The Chains of Psychological Slavery. In order to discover these traumatic syndromes, theological and philosophical speculations will not help. But rather, critical hermeneutical incisive-ness will unearth for us the traumatic syndromes the slaves suffered. I shall also rely on Diachronical Histographical and Diacritical evidence. In a number of cases African-descendants still suffers from these syndromes today with the reiteration legacies. We see these also in the diacritical histographical literatures, records, of the transatlantic legacies affecting African-descendants. The immediate effects are delineated in the psychological spheres, political spheres, social spheres, economical spheres, theological spheres and the cultural spheres. It is evident with the almost unbridgeable gulf of disconnection. Psychological disconnection. Social disconnection. Political disconnection. Economical disconnection.

I shall rely on diacritical and diachronic sources through the history of the heinous transatlantic "African" slave trade. The source particularly of the conscious programmed active involvement of the major denominations. Methodist, Anglican, Catholic, United Reformed, Baptist, Moravian and Presbyterian. Their focus was concentrated on the dis-empowerment of the African race racially. Indeed, the driving philosophy of the slave trade was the creation of permanent dis-empowerment of the black race. The churches began by not tolerating any form of African culture, customs, traditions and religious practices as acceptable on the plantations. The obliteration completely of Africanism was their motive. But this was not all. The dis-placement of all forms and relations of Africanism with the forced inculcation of Europeanism and British-ethno-centricism. Semantical-cultural-white Christianity. In a nutshell only, that which was European and British was acceptable. African tribal and ancestorial names were rejected and replaced. The rejection of Africanism was social, political, religious, economical, psychological and spiritual. The rejection was also anthropological. Men, women and children were sodomonized. Africans were denied their nature and composition of humanity. Africans were defined as non-being. They were defined as biologically ordained for slavery. The churches made also theological affirmation and justification for the enslavement of Africans. Africans were seen as chattels and beasts of burden without a soul. Missionaries described Africans as pagans and savages. Africans were looked at as uncivilized by whites coming to redeem the uncivilized Africans. By all accounts and elucidations the slaves suffered a dramatic physical, cultural, religious and spiritual excortication of their being human. They were defined as non-being. Dr. Runoko Rashidi reminds us that in 1967 the Aborigines were regarded as "non-beings." In the case of the story of the "Loss Generation" of Aborigines children, it was the Catholic Church, the Methodist and the Anglican Church which all agreed with the Government for the obliteration of this unique and ancient original natives of Australia.

The churches were the political presidium of the British Parliament. The slave trade merchants. The slave trade planters and enslavers. Slavery was an institution managed by the churches. Theologically the churches developed a theology where they claimed that Slavery was consistent with Christianity. Furthermore the missionaries claimed that God created Africans to be (a) Slaves. (b) So that the whites could convey salvation to Africans. Evangelization and Christianization were the churches modus operandi. This was the postulation of Prof. Roger Anstey in his book The Atlantic slave trade and British abolition 1760-1810. Prof. Anstey's moral and theological prevarication was that the enslavement of Africans was in line with God's "Salvation History". Here is theological justification of a cultural semantical Christianity without any significant integrity in contents and authority.

My central approach and philosophy to this thesis is based on the philosophy of Pan-Africanism. The embracement of the founding fathers of Pan-Africanism as illustrious and prodigious paradigms of inspirations worthy of emulation. Prof. Anne C. Bailey academically reminds us in her book "African Voices of the Atlantic Slave Trade" Beyond the Silence and the Shame." The modern concept of Pan-Africanism---or the unity of the African continent and it's Diaspora—germinated from the political philosophy of Trinidadian George Padmore (1901-59). (Malcolm Nurse) The International African Opinion of Jamaican-born Marcus Garvey, and other African- American scholar and activist

Dr. W.E.B. DuBoris, C .L .R. James, Henry Sylvester Williams. Pan-Africanism was concretized by Kwame Nkrumah the first President of Independent Ghana in 1957. These were the vanguards of black liberation.

Pan-Africanism is inclusive of all African-Caribbean descendants. This is profoundly psychological, cultural, social, economical, genealogical, political and theological. Babism for Africans is significant socially, politically and economically. These must be acknowledged universally in order for unity, acceptance and the radical psychological extirpation and dissipation of Europeans and British historical inculcations of stultification and negativism. Inculcation especially towards African allo-theism which was deep Cosmology of which African Myalism was a powerful manifestation of the Cosmic Mind which is united with the black spirit individually and collectively of the Black Jesus of the Black experience. How else did the slaves preserved and survived brutal slavery. The slaves survived because of their propinquity spiritually with God. This God in terms of morality was different from the cultural God of Europeans and British.

Slavery for the British was an institution of economic power. Cultural hegemony in the world. While slavery for the Africans and ex-slaves such as Ottobah Cugoano described by him in his book Thoughts and Sentiments on the Evils of Slavery (1787) Ignatius Sancho- Letters of the Late Ignatius Sancho An African, Olaudah Equiano, Authentic Narratives and James Albert Gronniosaw 1770- A Narrative of the Most Remarkable Particulars in the Life of James Albert Ukawsaw Gronniosaw, An African Prince as Related by Himself. Dr. Srividhya Swaminathan said of Phillis Wheatley that " her poetry resonated on several levels by defying stereotypes of race and gender and providing abolitionists like Granville Sharp with powerful evidence against racial stereotypes of African slaves." Slavery was for them the human embodiment of hate, evilness, racism and moralized cruelty. Paradoxically Slavery was based on Racism and economic philosophy of Rapacity and Superiority by Europeans and British alike.

It should not be problematic to see the impact of the various traumas the slaves suffered. The tabulation and chronology of these diacritical existential-empirical struggles of African-descendants are real. I begin with the first traumatic syndrome.

Chapter 3
Post Traumatic Slave Syndromes

First: Excoriation Traumatic Syndrome

According to the biblical creation story in the book of Genesis, God created all the creatures on earth and in the seas. But God it is said created man in his own image. The philosophers, the theologians and legal experts of the avaricious transatlantic (Black African) slave trade all said "except Africans." Even the US Constitution says Dr .Walter Rodney declared that man was created in the "Image of God" but did not include the Black race. Thomas Jefferson in drafting the American Constitution excluded Africans from sharing in "Liberty and Equality" while he fathered children with slave women. The Black man says "I am God because the God who created me I know that God but the European and British God of oppression, exploitation and injustice I do not know. Equally, the Black Jesus of the Black experience. Here is where culture and religion are at a great divide. How can the oppressor, those of hate, racism and cruelty interpret and defined God for the Black race? No, white philosophers and theologians cannot and they should not be allowed to do that nonsense on interpretations any longer. Europeans and British claimed that God made Africans for their slaves. They also claimed theological justification for the enslavement of Africans. Africans must see, understand and relate to God from their situational context. The Suffering God of the African race. The impregnated God that heard the groans and cries of his sons and daughters in the dungeons at Cape Coast Castle Ghana West Africa. On the slave ships. In the Middle Passage. In the hulls of the ships. In the violations of African women. In their rapes. In the sodomnization of African slaves in the name of a white God and a white Jesus Christ. The white churches saw no incongruity between enslavement of Africans and their white semantical-cultural-Christianity Exodus 6.V 1-9. The traumatic syndrome is permeating the Black Race without abatement. The British philosophical and theological schools never thought that the slave trade would be anathema. Both schools produced sagacious arguments that responded to public perceptions of the morality and legality of the slave trade.

God in his creation has empowered the Black race with beauty, dignity and humanity. That made us children of God. Appointed by God with the commission that we are called upon to worship God. To lift up His name with righteousness and the fear of God. To respect the Holiness of God. To seek justice and truth. Only a child and children of God can know these revelations of God. Not the slave masters, Planters, Merchants and enslavers. Not Rev'd. John Newton. Not William Wilberforce.

God in his creation bestowed on the African race "freedom". God never made Africans to be slaves in the bondage of slavery. As Mary Prince said "To be free is very sweet." Slavery was a violation of God's nature and purpose. It was an affront to God. It disturbed the heart (leb) of God. "I have surely seen the affliction of my people which are in (Egypt), Cape Coast Castel dungeon. And I have heard their cry by reason of their taskmasters: for I know their sorrows. And I am come down to deliver them up out of the land (Slavery) unto a good land and a large, unto a land flowing with milk and honey (Africa) Exo.3.7-8 All Black eyes and hopes should be on mother Africa. It is Africa that gave life to mankind. It is Africa that gave Science to the world. It is Africa that gave (God) religion to the world. The Black Jesus Christ will return to Africa. And Africa must be ready like a bride to receive our Black Jesus Christ at his Parousia. At that time there will be no more starvation, famine and suffering in Africa. All will be well before The Diaspora, Political Unification of Africa and Pan- Africanism movement will see and experience the Black Jesus in the revolution to liberate Africa from the technological hold of Europe, Britain and the USA.

Excoriation is the heinous and immoral removal of all properties and characteristics of being human to Africans. To say to the Africans your are non-being. You are pagans and you have no soul. This is the beginning of the Excoriation Traumatic Syndrome. To be called chattel.. My property. To remove all human rights. To remove all aspects of human dignity, personal, individual and collective. This was a devastation physically, emotionally, spiritually and psychologically of African descendants.

Second: Animalized Traumatic Syndrome

During the Apartheid evil system whites entombed their dogs and inscribed their names on tombs. Blacks were given only numbers. The same was during the slave trade plantation regime. Slaves had numbers and it was a common policy to re-named the slaves. It was to give the slaves what Dr.W.E. B. Dubois called “double consciousness”. And Dr. Srividhya Swaminathan called “diasporic identity”. The slaves were psychologically controlled by the whip and fear of the slaves masters power. The bodies of slaves some alive and some dead were placed on trees for the crows. Three things crippled the slaves. 1) chains. 2) shackles and 3) mantraps. Prof. Bailey reminds us that “mantraps” was used to literally break not only the physical but the spiritual will of the slaves because of the harshness of the punishment. These were the deeds and actions of Europeans and British Church leaders and members with the Bible in one hand and the guns made and supplied by the Quakers in the other hand.

I visited Ghana many years ago when I was researching for my published book European Christianity and the Atlantic Slave Trade. At Cape Coast Castle I perambulated (walked around) the castle. I stood in the dungeon. I felt the spirits of the African ancestors, brothers, sisters, mothers. fathers, sons and daughters. I was "inundated" over whelmed with inner pain. The feeling of connection was tremendous. I was so profoundly moved that I raised the theological question in my mind. Where was the omnipresence and omnipotence of God in the suffering of Africans in the dungeon? Why? On top of the dungeon is the Catholic Church Communion Table- where they celebrated the Eucharist. (Synaxis) The presence of the major churches mentioned already disturbed my theological concepts. I kept asking theological and philosophical questions. In this context of slavery- Does God exist? The Western philosophical arguments for the existence of God are meaningless arguments. "The Teleological, Cosmological and Ontological."

In July 2009 the United States of America President Barack Obama visited Ghana. He was taken to Cape Coast Castle. Mr. Anderson Cooper of CNN in his report of the President's visit made a special report on the history of the Castel and the conditions the slaves were placed in. To my deep amazement because I stood in the dungeon where President Obama stood." Mr. Cooper said "In 2008 some American Archaeologists investigated the dungeon. They carefully excavated the floor of the dungeon. They discovered that the floor was not concrete.

It was 12ins of (shit) faeces built up over the many years of holding the slaves before facing the unknown transatlantic crossing into slavery. The Middle Passage: The capacity of the dungeon was the holding of men, women and children for months. This was the beginning of Animalized Traumatic Syndrome. All in the name of a white Almighty God, Cultural Semantical Christianity and in the name of a white Jesus Christ. Remember the liturgy of the Eucharist celebration above the dungeon. (Do this in remembrance of me) (Synaxis) British and European Christianity was deeply fallacious commixed with fallibilism. William St. Clair in his book "The Grand Slave Emporium" Cape Coast Castle and the British Slave Trade. Described the Castle's condition and environment as "their heartlessness." or "psychic-distance." Cape Coast Castle was the headquarters of the British involvement in the transatlantic slave trade for 143 years. (1664-1807) It was described by one British governor as the "grand emporium of the British slave trade" The dungeon was the genesis for the slaves dehumanization and of the station of Animalized Traumatic Syndrome. The dungeon was the "Ephialtees" for all the slaves. It is psychologically and spiritually dominated their inner being in a endogenous physical manner.

Third: Dungeonization Traumatic Syndrome

To begin the long process to understand the physical, emotional, psychological and spiritual trauma of the dungeon, text books are not adequate. Books narrates the various accounts from documents and records. But to physically ambulate the dungeon convey a sense of evilness, feeling of sadness and dysteleology of life and humanity. It also beg the philosophical and theological question again, Does God Exist? Does God exists?

Dr. William St Clair in his book "The Door of NO Return" extrapolated from records described an extraordinary phenomena of 1651 " Perched on its rocks, isolated on its peninsula, and crammed with iron, Cape Coast Castle was frequently struck by lightning, as were the other European buildings on the coast. When Elmina Castle was struck in 1651 the governor reported that all the gold and silver melted but that the bags in which they were stored were not damaged. The swords were broken in their scabbards, which remained untouched. In the British slaving fort at Accra the walls were shattered and pewter vessels melted. In an age that had little or no understanding of electricity, such acts of God were terrifying and nobody knew what He i.e. God might do next.

Dr. William St Clair information is packed with details of the Castle and the dungeon. But one cannot fail with faith to perceive that God saw and heard the groans of those slaves dying in the dungeons. Are there theological grounds to support the attribute of God's ubiquity? Even so God's ubiquity would be meaningless without God's omnipotence in this concrete situation. Again the question is apt, does God exist? Those who had enslaved the Africans were people without conscience, morality, religious conviction of Africans equality and liberty. Although as mentioned before, there was and is the presence of the churches listed already at Cape Coast Castle. In the Dutch Reformed Church at Cape Coast there is the inscription in the church "God is in this place". It is necessary for a reiteration of theological context with significance here that the British were always historically "pagans". They were never Christians. The Dark Age is confirmation of this fact that the British is historically connected to the Dark Age. Semantical-cultural-Christianity was based on irreligious beliefs and traditions. It was based on European and British racism.

In the dungeon, men, women and children were imprisoned for weeks with only two small holes to let in air and light. The dungeon is below sea level with one entrance. Daily the dead bodies were removed and dumped in the sea. Africans religiously maintained a rigid respect for their dead. This must have had an additional impact on the already dungeonization traumatic syndrome. It had profound spiritual and psychological impacts.

No separate apartment for the women and children. No exit for human excrement. The slaves had no place to lay, even animals are allowed space to lay. The condition was that the slaves were animals. Rather than fearing God the Churches theology and preaching was the theological affirmation that Christianity and African enslavement was consistent with British Semantical Cultural Christianity. Paradoxically they saw no incongruity between Christianity and Slavery. The stench was more revolting and repugnant than Olaudah Equiano existential and empirical account and description of the hull of the slave ships.

Mr. Joseph Andoh Quarm in his book "African Concepts of God Human Being and Society. Know who God is, who you are, and why Society. Though he writes from the philosophical avenue of Nzema school of philosophical thought he emphasised the importance of the Supreme Being, Human and Society. He summarized Nzema effeminate power through the "Sacredness of Life". God is Supreme Being. Let me expand more on the dungeonization traumatic syndrome.

Elmina Castle Cape Coast is the largest of over 53 castles along the shore-region. At Elmina the community of enslavers, missionaries and chaplains and the ministers they were all pagans. They were heathens clothed in a racialised Christian semantical culture. The Africans had a profound awareness of the cosmological Supreme Being whilst the

British only knew economical avariciousness for the moral-less empire. Their economical rapacity and superior culture.

Prof. Bailey continued her observations and critique thus. "From the beginning of the European encounter with the African continent, economic prospects for Africa were tied to the notions of a religious crusade. Christianity was often used to justify slave traffic and traders like Barbot who rationalized his part in the horrible business by claiming that "Africans would then be able to receive the ultimate salvation". She says, "Most of the slave forts in Ghana had chapels next to the dungeons where slaves were kept like sardines awaiting slave ships. The chaplains job was to give their blessings to the sale in African slaves." The dungeonization traumatic syndrome was further created by the nature and environment of the dungeon. Anthony Tibbles summarization of the slaves condition is appropriate here. "They often faced long arduous journey and few knew what final destination or fate awaited them. On arrival at the coast they were usually imprisoned in forts before being loaded on to ships. Few would have ever seen the sea or a ship or a white man before.

They found themselves thrown together with people from different parts of Africa, speaking different languages, in condition of horror, deprivation and violence. In this way they crossed the Atlantic." "Middle Passage." The dungeonization traumatic syndrome was a continuation of the demographical psychological randomization traumatic syndrome. The slaves began therefore, with a double dose of dehumanization.

Fourth: Infibulations Traumatic Syndrome

Prof. James Walvin book "Britain's Slave Empire" the cover delineating a picture of the hull of a slave ship carrying slaves. Prof. Herbert S. Klein book “The Atlantic Slave Trade” page 146 also shows pictures of slaves packed like sardines head to toe with a space of only 18ins. This is how the slaves were taken across the mighty Atlantic (African) slave trade passage. It was a Traumatic Syndrome and Olaudah Equiano described for us existentially and empirically the conditions of “Infibulations” in his book “The Interesting Narrative and other Writings.”

.

Fifth: Imbrications Traumatic Syndrome

Greed was the driving force behind the slave trade, what Aunt Charlotte called the” iron heel of “slavery” Dr. Ann C Bailey called it “the Ruthless Efficiency”. Full capacity was a basic norm with the aid of the slave ship doctor and the slave ship chaplain. These Traumatic Syndromes caused the slaves tremendous confusion and pummelled the slaves psychologically and spiritually.

Sixth: Demographical Psychological Traumatic Syndrome

The aggressive deracination and bringing together of different groups on the slave ships and unto the different plantations. This is where there was heightened heterogeneity. The conflicts were astonishing to say the least. Demographical Psychological Randomization Traumatic Syndrome was the environment for confusion, consternation, depression and bewilderment. It was psychologically and spiritually imperious. It was as in the dungeon, the linguistic moment of confusion. Their only commonality was their skin colour, the skin and the shared experience of enforced enslavement. Thereby making the slaves comprehensively disempowered and dehumanized.

Seventh: Stultification Traumatic Syndrome

Women were raped at random. They were sexed openly on the plantations. Boys and Girls were auctioned at age 3yrs. So-called husbands had to watched their wives being sexually abused in their presence by the slave masters, their sons and friends. Husbands wives were forcefully taken from them and hired out to other masters and friends for sexual gratifications. They pulverised the slave women dignity and womanhood. They were categorized like animals on a farm. The slaves had no humanity. The traumatic syndromes functioned at different levels even without diffidence because they were disempowered. But it was their combined suffering that gave them the catag-matic unified spirit of a fractured life but not only life but human spirit.

Eighth: Routinization Traumatic Syndrome

The slaves lives were hell on earth. The missionaries audaciously preached hell damnation to the slaves, should they talk or seek their freedom. Submission to slavery was their lot in order to get milk and honey in the after-life. The Methodist was excellent in this form of preaching and inculcation. Routinization was the basic truncation of the slaves spirit. But theologically and cosmologically the slaves had a relationship with God that was profoundly meaningful. Mary Prince experience is a valid quotation.

"How can slaves be happy when they have the halter round their neck and the whip upon their back? And are disgraced and thought no more than beasts? And are separated from their mothers, and husbands, and children, and sisters, just as chattels are sold and separated? Is it happiness for a driver in the field to take down his wife or sister or a child, and strip them, and whip them in such a disgraceful manner?—women that have had children exposed in the open field to shame. There is no modesty or decency shown by the owner to his slaves; men, women, and children are exposed alike. Since I have been here I have often wondered how English people can go out into the West Indies and act in such a beastly manner. But when they go to the West Indies, they forget God and all sense of shame. I think, since they can see and do such things... All slaves want to be free—to be free is very sweet. I will say the truth to English people who may read this history that my good friend, Miss S---, is now writing down for me. I have been a slave myself—I know what slaves feel—I can tell myself what other slaves feel, and by what they have told me." Captives and Countrymen. Barbary Slavery and the American Public. 1785-1816. Lawrence A. Peskin. 2009.

There were no physical changes in conditions for the slaves. They were born into slavery, lived as slaves and died as slaves. Their routinization traumatic syndrome dominated their composition. Dis-empowerment from religion, customs, traditions, freedom, country. Family, traditional gods and ancestorial spirits. Such truncation and separation of the human spirit in the bondage of slavery.

Ninth: Suboptimization Traumatic Syndrome

Prof. Roger Anstey defined the transatlantic "African" slave trade as a "dynamic system." It was this dynamic system that the slaves could not come to terms with. It was a system of moral repugnancy according to Prof. James Walvin. Manumission was now an epistemological dream for the slaves. The plantation was for the slaves their alpha and omega. Their birth and their death.

The transatlantic (African) slave trade system was designed for the permanent creation of dis-empowerment of all Africans. This intension affects the African Diaspora. Connection becomes an academic subject. There is a universal connection throughout the Diaspora. African descendants shared a profligate brutal enslavement experience. It is therefore "sincere ignorance" of the highest order when some

African-Caribbean people refused to acknowledge that they have a shared historical connection. African-descendants must remember that education was based on what the British stipulated. It was in line with their colonization structure and the perpetuation of dis-empowerment of all African descendants. They claimed that slavery was abolished, however economical and political determination was still ultimately British and European.

Tenth: Brutalization Traumatic Syndrome

The illustrious and immortal Frederick Douglas was the first slave to have used the word "brutalization" to described his existential and empirical life as a slave. In Chapter XV11 (The Last Flogging) writing on the contents of this moving chapter. A Sleepless night-Return to Covey's-Pursued By Covey-The Chase Defeated-Vengeance. Postponed-Musing in The woods-The Alternative-Deplorable. Spectacle-Night in the woods-expected attack-Accosted By Sandy, A friend, not a hunter-Sandy's Hospitality- The "Ash Cake" supper-The interview with Sandy-His Advice-Sandy A conjurer as well. As a Christian – The Magic Root-strange meeting with Covey-His manner-Covey's Sunday Face-Author's Defence- Resolve-The fight-the victory, and its results. Frederick Douglas described his short fugitive life and his spontaneous return to his master. The physical fight he had; and his physical power over his master, which immediately transformed his slave life. But it is to be admitted that Olaudah Equiano (Gustavus Vassa) who was converted to Methodism and became an outspoken opponent of the slave trade also frequently made reference to the slave trade as brutality mixed with racism.

Eleventh: Dehumanization Traumatic Syndrome

The literary and intellectual capacities of Afrikans during the transatlantic slave trade had never been above that of the animals. Reverend Robert Boucher writes in 1888 "The stupidity of negroes is urged by the friends of slavery as a plea for using them as brutes; for they represent the negroes as little removed above the monkey, or the oranoutang, with regard to intellects. But I am very certain, nothing has been written by the late defenders of slavery that discovers (displays) half the literary merit or ability of two Negro writers. Phillis Wheatley wrote correct English poetry within a few years after her arrival in Boston from Afrika; and there is a Latin ode of considerable length written in classic language by Francis Williams… I never heard of poems by a monkey, or of Latin odes by an oranoutang."

Dr. Helen Thomas writing in her book- Romanticism Slave Narratives Transatlantic Testimonies presented Phillis Wheatley in all her prodigious glory. Dr. Thomas said of Thomas Jefferson. Jefferson described Wheatley's work as a product of religious enthusiasm rather than of poetic talents. "Misery is often the parent of the most affecting touches in poetry. Among the black is misery enough, God knows, but no poetry. Love is the peculiar oestrum of the poet. Their love (blacks) is ardent, but it kindles the senses only, not the imagination. Religion indeed, has produced a Phillis Wheately (sic); but it could not produce a poet. The compositions published under her name are below the dignity of criticism."

Dr. Thomas elucidating says that in this text, Jefferson described Wheatley's work as a product of religious enthusiasm rather than poetic talent. Whilst Jefferson's remark demonstrates the coalescence of ethnographic studies with theoretical justification of slavery, it must be remembered that Wheately's poetical work presented an encroachment of the autobiographical forum presided over by Jefferson, a site which conflated the dynamics of autobiography with those of cultural ideology and 'nation' writing.

Phillis Wheately work "Poems on Various Subjects, Religious and Moral" was a tremendous challenge to racism. The slave trade and slavery as an institution. Abolition of Slavery and Emancipation. Both Equiano and Granville Sharp were deeply impressed with her work and they used her work in the abolition struggles. In addition her poems emphasised the inalienable rights of all humans to personal liberty as explicated in the theological, philosophical and political theories of Locke, Hume and Montesquieu. It is significant to note here that The London Chronicle declared the poet an infant prodigy of pronounced linguistic and cultural talent.

Prof. James Walvin writing in his "Black Ivory. A History of British Slavery" reminds us that slaves were seen and treated as brutes. Rev. William Davis of Antigua was not only Anglican minister and manager of slave property but he was indicted for the murder of Wliza, a slave woman. Larry D. Crawford posed for us the question of the (death marches) of slaves for a thousand miles. "Imagine being forced to urinate, defecate or vomit while walking?" Dr. Lawrence A Peskin writing in his book "Captives and Countrymen- Barbary Slavery and the American Public" 1785-1816 said that in the eyes of Foss the "ultimate death of an Afrikan Christian is nothing more thought of, by the inhabitants, than the death of one of their domestic animals." The Rev. John Smith (Methodist minister) dispatched to Demerara in 1816, was told "not a word must escape you in public or private which might render the slaves displeased with their masters or dissatisfied with their station. You are sent not to relieve them from their servile condition, but to afford them the consolation of religion." According to Dr. Walvin, in time, these consolations were to prove temporal as much as spiritual.

Twelfth: Desideratum Traumatic Syndrome

Africans were brutally captured and physically and sexually abused. The slaves were chained to each other. Here lies the heterogeneity of differences and hatred. The slaves were then dungeon- zed in the physical confinement of the dungeons. Their journey is described thus: "Slaves had to trudged past already gorged animals leisurely picking and choosing and feeding off the collection of fresh and decomposing bodies and skeletal remains of one out of every three Africans who had been chained and beaten down this trail of blood and tears." Equiano's account of the slaves on the slave ship and his own condition is vividly articulated in his moving book. Interesting Narratives. At the International Slavery Museum in Liverpool there are technological dramatizations of the Middle Passage what Crawford called the "Great Suffering or Maafa." In other words the "Great Destruction." The slaves dreamed and desired to return to Africa where they had the greatest blessing from God, namely "freedom." The plantations, the dungeons and barracoons experiences were all based on desideratum traumatic syndromes.

In this significant chapter mentioned above, Frederick Douglas reached the zenith of his struggles and life at sixteen. Although he was advised by Sandy, yet he was divinely inspired to fight for his inner physical and psychological liberation. There is some measure of divine comparison between Douglas and the biblical Moses. Douglas physically fought his oppressor Convey and won. He regained his manhood and humanity against Convey's brutality. The case I have been describing, was the end of the "ratification" to which slavery subjected me." "I was nothing before; I was a Man Now. It recalled to life my crushed self-respect and my self-confidence, and inspired me with a renewed determination to be a Freeman. A man, without force, is without the essential dignity of humanity. Human nature is so constituted, that it cannot honour a helpless man, if the signs of power do not arise."

The physical and psychological basis and function of the transatlantic slave trade was based on physical brutality, psychological destruction of the slaves and domination of the slaves lives. Whilst Douglas described his life as a slave with brutalization, Olaudah Equiano in his "The Interesting Narrative of the Life of Olaudah Equiano." Equiano portrayed his European captors as "satanic demons and their ship as "a hellish nightmare." Lawrence A. Peskin in his book "Captives and Countrymen-Barbary Slavery and the American Public. 1785-1816" Says. "Equiano wrote his narrative to a large part as antislavery propaganda at a time when there was growing abolitionist sentiment throughout the Atlantic world. By pointing out the barbaric un-Christian behaviour of the European captors, he hoped to shame them into renouncing their role as slaveholders."

The Middle Passage: "Kebuka" Remembering the Middle Passage Through the Eyes of our Ancestors is a quotation from Dr. Amos N. Wilson. "Simply because we choose to forget a traumatic event, simply because we choose not to learn of a traumatic history and a history that may make us feel ashamed, does not mean that history is not controlling our behaviour."

One of the most profound things that we've learned in psychology is that the most powerful forces that shape human behaviour are those factors that are consciously not remembered by human beings, that are unknown by the person, are those experiences the individual can swear he's never had. That is one of the paradoxes of human behaviour, that the very things that shape us and make us behave the way we do, see the world the way we see it and relate to people the way we relate to them, are those things that occurred in our lives at points we cannot remember or recall."

Chapter 4
African-Caribbean Diffidence and Impuissance

The disempowerment of African-Caribbean descendants must be approached from the diachronical perspective. In order to begin to understand the historical traumas the subject cannot be looked at in a laodiecon manner. Spiritual and intellectual attitudes of exfidefortis (strong spirit) is a compulsory requirement. The traumatic syndromes are a continuation of the process of disempowerment. These are now outlined as follows.

1) Racialisation Traumatic Syndrome

Missionaries, Slave Traders, Merchants, Politicians. Theologians and Philosophers applied a racialisation policy to the slaves. Their policy was theological and cultural. Their moral responsibility was with God. God had intended the enslavement and disempowerment of Africans. Even when such claims are deeply mendacious and cultural, they sought justification theologically by Christianization and Evangelization. Africans had no acculturalization but their culture was forcefully replaced, by the abandonment of names, customs, social habits, food, religion and family ties .These were repudiated by enslavement. Enslavement was disempowerment, the taking away of Africans rights and humanity. Property-ship was the philosophy legally and economic programme for the economy of Britain, Europe and America.

Despite the racialisation, the African-Caribbean Diaspora remained disempowered in all departments of life. Deracialization was the common approach of the Theologians, Historians based on an endemic disrespect for the humanity of Africans. It is a legacy of titanic force and power facing all African-Caribbean people. The warrant-ability is the combination of self-esteem and collective consciousness connection. Disempowerment and enslavement caused the evacuation of all qualities ontologically relating to being by the Supreme Being we call God.

2) Spiritualization Traumatic Syndrome

Prof. Anne C. Bailey described the Middle Passage journey of the Atlantic slave trade that it was understood in physical terms – shackles; whips and large numbers of Africans, slaves packed like sardines in small holes, tears; and the dead strewn in the midst of the living. But Prof. Bailey has progressed theologically to a spiritual Everest when she says "What would Africans who in traditional societies acknowledged the sacred in every sphere of life and particularly at the point of death do in the face of such sacrilege? For people who upheld such strong and abiding beliefs in the power of the ancestors and in the reincarnation of ancestral spirits, not to be able to bury their dead according to the proper rites and most importantly in the proper place must have been as devastating as the loss of their freedom" Myalism., pantheism and henotheism survived the vicissitudes of the whole transatlantic (African) slave trade period of 500 years. The only survivable diacritical property is oral tradition or transmission. It was a deep spiritual, inner cultural and psychological victualing of the “Soul” which according to Socrates is immortal that impregnated the slaves inner spirit to live.

3) Villagization Traumatic Syndrome

Diachronical histographical displacement of the slaves not only affected their physical being but the effects penetrated into the spiritual, psychological, individual and communal togetherness, customs, freedom, village symbiotic responsibility of the elders and chiefs including the paramount chiefs. It was not a matter of bringing the slaves into demographic urbanity. It was the complete deracination from, villagization into bondage. The bondage of enslavement and the transportation across the Atlantic to Brazil, America and the Caribbean regions. The truncation created Villagization Traumatic Syndrome not recoverable physically. It embodied at the same-time disempowerment because the slaves no longer had a voice. Forced submission brutally and by brainwashing. The Bible in one hand and the gun in the other. At frequent times the whip.

4) Stultification Traumatic Syndrome

The slaves were reduced to the levels of chattels, property, random sex machine, young men and women placed together for the production of providing slave children like pigs, goats, cows and horses for the plantations and the slave master. Husbands had no right over his wife. The slave master has had all the rights. The bond between a mother and child is the strongest energy in life. Children were literally dragged from their mothers arms and carted away for auctions in the market places.

The slaves were told in the fashion of inculcation that Almighty God had designed them to be slaves. Their humanity and dignity were stripped. They were left with nothing. Even their breath was not wholesome. Life had no happiness and the promise of a bright tomorrow. The fundamental foundation of society was seriously dislocated namely the (Family).Without the family there is no community. There is no unified generation.

The Stultification Traumatic Syndrome is still damaging the young African-Caribbean people in Britain. Most now have a profound lack of self-esteem and a sense of worthlessness because of the education system. Vacant-esteem is a commonplace characterization of most African-descendant Blacks. Castigating failures of Central Government and Local Government. Serious moral failures of the churches in Britain. Stultification traumatic syndrome runs deep in the psyche of African-Caribbean people. It is so deep that it has become a common expectation to be stultified. To be a no body. To be a failure. Once again there is a potent message from the pen of Mary E. Modupe Kolawole. "Africans, however, attempted to revisit history through anthropological, archaeological, oral literary, oral historical and diverse other sources to objectify the experience and portray the transatlantic slave trade from the horse's mouth. To the African, the devastation suffered physically, psychologically, emotionally and morally almost defies atonement." In other words, disempowerment is cultural, spiritual, emotional and deeply psychological.

At the age of eighteen I was on my way to College. I met a Jamaican lady I knew from Jamaica. She pretended that she was happy to see me. Mrs. Bertha Milwood son what are you doing? I am going to College. To do what she said to me? I said shoe making. Very good boy. She walked away laughing. In actual fact I was a University student. A few years later she visited Jamaica. She met my parents. She proudly said to them. I met your son Robinson in London. He should be a good shoe maker by now. My parents were surprised. They said to her, you are mistaken. Our son finished his degree and he is doing further studies for the Methodist Ministry and Post-graduate studies at University. My point is this, African-Caribbean descendants have modicum expectations of their own. High expectations are hard to come by today.

I met the lady countless times in London. She was even a very good friend of my sister. We met at weddings and funeral services I conducted. She refused to acknowledged me again. Each time she saw me all she did was to fixed her eyes on me with anger in her eyes. This is the stultification traumatic syndrome expectation. Negativism and un-sublime-ness are the cultural common expectation of many African-Caribbean people.

African-Caribbean young people are in the stultification category and expectation. Society expects them to be worthless. Some agents in society make sure they have damaged character. That their records is very much blotted. Their future is amputated. Their chances are limited. There is a stain on their record. It is the stultification certification of worthlessness. Even the adults have this deep stultification traumatic syndrome expectation.

I went into Barclays Bank branch in Stoke Newington many years ago I joined the queue. Most of the customers were African-Caribbean people. Unknown to me, after I left the Bank a Jamaican woman began to shout loud in the Bank. That Methodist minister that was in here. I knew him when he was a little boy. Now he is driving a big car and rings on his fingers. Look at him. Her language was over bearing to the staff and customers. She had nothing positive to say about me all negative things. Her attitude was so bad, that the white Bank manger called her to a counter and said to her, Lady, the time you are taking to say all those negative things about the minister, why don't you go and work hard like the minister and become somebody?" Her gripe was. I had surpassed her stultification traumatic syndrome expectation.

5) Separation Traumatic Syndrome

Slaves were separated from their immediate families. The separation had no consultation and social agreement. It was done at random despite the religious, social, political, domestic and economical situation. The purpose was the number of slaves for the rapacity of an economic culture based on economical superiority. But there is another dimension to the situation. The separation was permanent in that the slaves had no dignity or power. Endemic in the physical and psychological spheres of separation there is deep powerlessness.

6) Disconnection Traumatic Syndrome

The traumatic syndromes have a high degree of dis- connectedness because there are philosophically endless links and relationships even without .a relationship. People are connected or disconnected psychologically and spiritually.

7) Barracoonization Traumatic Syndrome

The barracoons were large buildings built by the slaves themselves. It was the slaves dwellings. The slaves had been defined as beast of burden created by God to be slaves. Christianity and a white Jesus Christ approved slavery. The slaves dissipated their normal waste like animals in one side of the holding. Within the barracoons there were separate sections for breeding slaves. The system worked this way.

The enslavers would at random looked for the youthful robust men between 18years and 25years. These were the fittest. They were at their most productive age, (The age for breeding) They were extracted and uprooted from their family, friends and fatherland. In all this says Mary E. Modupe Kolawole writing on "An African View of Transatlantic Slavery and the Role of Oral Testimony in Creating a New Legacy. Transatlantic Slavery Against Human Dignity. "In all this, women as mothers felt the agony more profoundly. The lure of better conditions in Europe and the Americas was not justified by attendant emotional, physical and psychological trauma and dehumanization." Some women tried to escape or commit suicide as an alternative to degradation and dehumanization. Women also constituted a formidable force in attacks on barracoons because of the breeding purpose. Men and women had to be physically very tall and at their peak condition. These young men were the baracoon stallions. The young men were looked upon to be the pedigree bulls. The rapid breeding of the young women transformed them into hopeless effeminate chattels. (effete) The women were not placed with one man in the sense of monogamous living. Several young men serviced her until she became pregnant. The woman had no choice, she was considered a young breeding dog, pig, goat or mare. The men through humiliation were deeply effeminized. When a man is effeminized it is the ultimate degree of psychological and physical stultification.

The enslavers next task was the choosing of the best and fittest young girls. Their age had to be like the young men 18 years to 25 years.

Once this task was done they were forced to sleep together for breeding purposes. Should the woman failed to breed, she would be taken back onto the plantations. Women who got pregnant but with the brutality of slavery refused to carry their pregnancy were severely castigated with the whip. She would be whipped and forced to abort the foetus

.Barracoonization was brutal. It was dehumanization of the slaves. It was degrading and heartless for the slaves.
Baracoonism was a traumatic syndrome because the whole exercise was slavery for all Africans. Another dimension of the barracoon plantation policy was the breeding of slaves in order to improve the economic power of the merchants and enslavers.

8) Racialisation Traumatic Syndrome

It is a fundamental fact of the transatlantic (African) slave trade that the slavery was based on racism. In other words because the enslaved were Africans. Stephen Small writing on The General Legacy of the Atlantic Slave Trade under the subheading of racialisation and racist ideologies says. The scientist insisted on the vilification of the Africans and their inferiority. They used science and philosophy to justify oppression, exploitation and injustice. Small reminds us of the racist David Hume the philosopher. "I am apt to suspect the negroes and in general all other species of men to be naturally inferior to whites. There never was a civilized nation of any complexion than white nor even any individual eminent in action. No ingenious manufacturer among them, no arts, no sciences. There are negro slaves dispersed all over Europe of which none ever displayed any symptoms of ingenuity." (David Hume -1734) It was Dr. Eric Williams in his thesis British Historians and the West Indies who dissipated David Hume theory in his essay of National Characters written in 1753. David Hume was blinded by his own racism. He could not have read or heard of St. Augustine. Phillis Wheately, James Albert Ukawsaw Gronniossaw, Equiano and Sancho.

Racialisation Traumatic Syndrome like all the traumatic syndromes are both traceable into the transatlantic (African) slave trade. But it is self-evident and diacritical that African descendants live every day with the perpetual reiteration legacies of slavery and racism. The vocabulary may have changed but the effects and legacies are constant re-memory for African descendants.

I have examined some of the major traumatic syndromes suffered by the slaves. There effects are within the same degree of pain, suffering, humiliation and indignity experienced by Black people. All the traumatic syndromes are visible among African descendants whether all African descendants are aware of these or not. They are parts of the consciousness of the psychological framework and function of African descendants. Nonetheless, the culmination of the various syndromes lies within the complexity of the traumatic dis-connection syndrome. This is the major problem, historically and more so today as we see the so-called developed world expanding and Africa and counties with African- descendants of colour are moving far away from the margin of survival. Poverty and injustice are pandemic.

9) Pummelled Traumatic Syndrome

Over the past 35-40 years the Transatlantic (African) slave trade: has generated tremendous academic scholarships and books that are at the point of inundations. Sadly, although some of the British major Universities such as Cambridge and Oxford have research facilities of significance. Others in their history department have been paying very little attention to the imperative subject. The whole environment of Europe, Britain and North America are linked historically to that economical developments of the Transatlantic (African) slave trade.

It is with admission that the Theological Colleges in Britain have not made the Transatlantic (African) slave trade a major academic subject. These colleges are training potential ministers for Circuits and

Parish ministries especially among Africans and African-Caribbean descendants. How can they being part of the historical lineage of the effects, impacts and legacies of the transatlantic (African) slave trade be effective theologically and pastorally? Stephen Small is worthy of full quotation here. "For the last 500 years the countries of the West have relentlessly exploited Africa and African people. Millions of Africans were murdered. Millions more violently kidnapped and enslaved, women raped and brutalised, and African societies totally ransacked. Slavery and colonialism were carried out for the economic enrichment of the West, with the full legal and political sanction and approval of Presidents, Prime Ministers, Royals, Parliament and the major church leaders.

The International Slavery Museum at the Merseyside Maritime Museum in Liverpool is a visible link in the painful psychological and physical dislocation of all African descendants. The Slavery Museum creates that deep connection which had been truncated, suppressed, negated, denied, re-interpreted most frequently not by African descendants students and scholars, but mainly white scholars from the Americas, Europe and Britain. Valid passionate and intellectual connection academically is more meaningful with the people of the African Holocaust. African Diasporas.

Any physical perambulation of the International Slavery Museum cannot fail in its demonstration of the brutal enslavement of innocent African men, women and children into a slave system based on cultural superiority and economical rapacity and Racism. The slaves were trammelled as they were conditioned to slavery with all the evilness therein. One act of trammelled impact was the "branding" of the slaves like horses and cows. A quick look at any of the American Western movies with the cow-boys and red-Indians will almost immediately convey the traumatic trammelled syndromes of the slaves. (The branding of the cows)

Chapter 5
Dr. Joy Leary and Dr. Akbar's postulations

I have valid appreciation for the contributions of both Dr. Leary and Dr. Akbar even where their contributions are based on social reflections of the African-American context. They complemented each other. But I am forced by the dynamics of the diacritical to look beyond their contributions. Dr. Joy Leary Post Traumatic Slave Syndrome and Dr. Akbar Historical Traumatic Syndrome. I have listed above the various traumatic experiences and conditions of the slaves over time. These additional traumatic syndromes I have both discovered through critical and jobsite patience, and thoughtfully formulated them and placed them situationally and contextually. Now, therefore, we are confronted by these diabolical traumatic syndromes which disempowered the slaves. We see and experience around us the germination and dissemination of the diseases and the multitude of reiteration legacies impacting especially on the African-descendants young people.

Physically, spiritually, socially, economically and politically we cannot separate ourselves from the past. In the Old Testament we make references always to the past. The God of our Fathers. We laudate Abraham, Isaac and Jacob. In the Eucharist we say in faith: "Drink this in remembrance of me. Take and eat it, in remembrance of Me." (Syntax's) Transatlantic (African) Slave Trade in Africans is engraved on African-Caribbean memory. It is in our very being. It is in our psyche. It is the big story of Africa. Slavery is Africa. Africa that was raped of its pedigrees and prodigious sons and daughters for free labour for European, British and American economies. The continent of Africa is still being raped today by foreign multi-national companies technologically. Many African leaders continue to see Africa on the cheap, because of self interest, rather than for the people and country. African-Caribbean people are deeply disempowered. Disempowerment is not only economical and political. It is educational, sociological, technological, scientific, agricultural, and collective-spirits. The only catagmatic link with Africa and the Diaspora is the transatlantic slave trade experiences, conditions and history. This historical and psychological, consciousness-connection links are efficacious for Pan-Africanism and the Diasporas.

The several traumatic syndromes I have written on above, they are not complete. There is much more analytical studies yet to be done. My findings and postulations are only ground-breaking findings. In order to find collective means to cope and transform meaningfully the ocean of disempowerment, individuals and little pockets of African-Caribbean people will not do. It requires collective efforts. It requires a profound sense of Pan-Africanism from a Diaspora dimension. Black academics and professionals are seriously guilty of dereliction to Pan-Africanism. In relation to the study of the Transatlantic (African) Slave Trade and all it impacts and ramifications on African-Caribbean descendants sociologically and psychologically.

The basis of the stultification traumatic syndromes are (a) deracination traumatic syndrome, and (b) Excortication traumatic syndrome. The forceful uprooting of communities into inhuman prisons. From their villages, social settings, and historical ties. The demographical psychological randomisation traumatic syndrome. African slaves were brutally conditioned into complete excortication of all features and characteristics of being human. The total reduction to non-being and chattels.

It follows naturally and consistently, that the second relationship and the effectuation of stultification is the excortication of the slave's dignity and humanity. Without dignity there is no humanity. It is the stripping away of the attributes ontologically provided by God like the barks of a tree. It is bare. It is fractured. It can no longer live. The bark is that which gives cover and protection. Slavery was the stripping and taking away of human qualities. It was the transformation of the human into non-being. From human to the beast of burden. It was the destruction of self-empowerment. The taking away of one's manhood and womanhood. (Effeminized) The taking away of womanhood. (effete) Both male and female were reduced into a world of dysteleology. A world of purposelessness. It was through exposures of the slaves. They had to bath in the sea openly. They were randomly sexed openly on the plantations. The primitive beast-like-ness of European and British men were in full projection. Slaves were beheaded at random for the exhibition of power and the creation of fear among the slaves. On Sundays they were in church singing "What a friend we have in Jesus." The Missionaries preached hell-fire and condemnation only to the slaves. It was the rapid spread of Christianization through evangelization culturally and semantically re-enforced for slavery.

Disempowerment is dysfunctionalism and paralysis. It is the source of dependence. We see both disempowerment and dependence in the developing world. The developing world is mainly African countries and descendants. Why? The transatlantic (Black African) slave trade philosophy was for the creation of permanent dis-empowerment of the peoples called Africans. The hateful racial enslavement of Africans was their psychological ephialtees. It was and is based on Racism and cultural Superiority. Even the United Nations Aids, and the different European and British Aids. The American Aids, these ethically are designed to perpetuate the continuation of permanent disempowerment of African countries and African descendants. It is the denial of manumission. It is political and technological slavery in the dress and form of modernism.

Chapter 6
Reparation Solidarity in Struggles

The fundamental aim and objective of the dynamic system of the transatlantic (Black African) slave trade was the creation of permanent disempowerment and powerlessness of Africans and African-Caribbean descendants. Looking critically and with the rectitude of honesty at the history of the slave trade and what the system had intended. African descendants are at the bottom of the economic world of development. Poverty, penury, is the evidence of injustice and general under-development is a living and walking companion with all African descendents. Reparation struggles has been on the move for a very, very long time. There are several movements and individuals past and present who had some measure of dialogue or engagement with the struggles for reparation. Their contributions must not be overlooked. But paradoxically, reparation is not only political with European, British and American governments. Reparation is inclusive of the Churches. Governments and Churches or Christianity are synonymous and politically entrenous for economical reasons.

On the British front in 1993 the late Bernie Grant MP helped to form the African Reparations Movement UK (ARM.) According to Mr. Grant the transatlantic slave trade in Africans was a genocide and crime against humanity. The uprootment and transportation of 280,000.000-300,000.000 Africans across the Atlantic Middle Passage. As a Liberation Theologian, I add strength to Bernie Grant basic thesis, that the transatlantic slave trade was an affront to global humanity and the belief in a moral and just God. But Bernie Grant claimed that colonisation. Oppression and enslavement of Africans was an extraordinary moral and physical crime committed in human history.

Africans are still suffering materially, environmentally, economically and most significantly psychologically. The zenith of Bernie Grant deep and veracious desire was that the European, British and American countries that raped Africa should build a railway across the whole of Africa—from north to south and east to west in order to provide the opportunity for internal and international trade. Africa according to Andrew Young must have the outlet to international markets. Reparation for Bernie Grant was to be for the irreparable damage to Africa sociologically, politically, economically and psychologically. These dreams might appear in dual ways, both as a chimerical dream or an epistemological dread. Any meaningful replacement of this dream must first come through political unification of the continent. Africa needs political-unification. In an age of economical, political, technological and cultural unification Africa needs political unification. The extirpation of the Berlin Conference 1884-85 minutes recorded and stipulated that Africa must be carved up into 53 countries for the cementation of European and British hegemony. Africans leaders and countries must consolidate and unite with political-unification. It is in this sphere that real empowerment and raising the consciousness lies.

According to Dr. Anne C. Bailey there has been different individuals verbalizing and articulating the need for “Reparation.” In Europe and Britain there has never been any productive symbiotic African-descendants movement with International Legal teeth. Such biting teeth must be economical, technological and political in order to create the environment for Reparation discussion for compensation. However, the matter is not for the International Courts for Human Rights, the United Nations or the political agenda of European, Britain and American governments. The urgent need is for African leaders and the Diasporas to start a global moral, social, cultural, political and psychological crusade. Failures in themselves as African leaders are a form of disempowerment and powerlessness because Africans leaders are not fully united. It is furthermore a visible sign of the absence of collective-connection-consciousness among African countries and the Diasporas. Reparation solidarity is not perspicuous sociological, economical and political to black political leaders. It is necessary to add also the psychological dimension. African leaders need psychological regeneration, and reintegration, plus cultural and psychological reorientation.

From the early 1990 African-descendants have been demanding reparations from the rich and developed nations of the West, for the injustice, exploitation perpetuated against Africa and African-descendants during the heinous period of slavery and colonialism. The major historical International Conference on the specific subject of Reparation took place in 1993 when Bernie Grant took part at the Conference in Abuja Nigeria. In attendance were distinguished academics and lawyers.

Reparations U.K. had a remarkable voice. The major appeal now is for the united states of American to support the volume of calls for Reparation. But the demand for reparation must be contextually correct. The compensation Britain made to the merchants and enslavers was £20,000.000. Likewise the French made reparation as well. The movement must be a moral force and argument. The French demanded from Independent Haiti, compensation and reparation to be recognized as an independent state. This was daylight skulduggery. It was dishonest. It is the fundamental cause of Haiti's poverty today. France is literally owing Haiti says Prof. Hilary Beckles (UWI) 150 million francs or US.21 billion. 24th January 2010.

It is necessary to point out two further significant points. First, the transatlantic slave trade was the economic foundation of Europe, Britain and the USA. Dr. Eric Williams made this very perspicuous in his thesis on Capitalism and Slavery. Reparation must be linked to the Berlin Conference of 1884-85. It was at this time that Europe and Britain carved up Africa into 53 countries to make their domination and hegemony over Africa more effective. Political-unification can be an integral part and function of the Reparation Solidarity Struggle for the continent of Africa.

Steven Small said in his book on Transatlantic Slavery Against Human Dignity. That Reparation is a legally enforced repayment for the damage and destruction caused by the immoral, morally repugnant and racialised Transatlantic (Black African) slave trade. Reparations were made by the German government to Israel for the Jewish victims of the Nazi Holocaust. Reparation were made by the United States government to the Japanese and Japanese Americans interned during World War 2. The failure of Europe, Britain and the USA in not making reparation to Africa and the Caribbean is a direct continuation of Racism, In-equality and Injustice.

At the heart of the African experience is Racism. Every area of the slave trade had been marked by racism. Definitions, expectations, treatments, brutalization, oppression and exploitation with indignity for free African labour. The transatlantic (Black African) slave trade needs to be demanded to be kept on the moral conscience and agenda of the governments mentioned above. Reparation would be an acknowledgement of a moral evil and wrong done to innocent people (Africans). It would be a theological acknowledgement of the wrongs done by people who labelled themselves Christian-Missionaries, Anglican, Catholic, Methodist, Baptist, United Reformed, Quakers and Moravian Churches.

I would not advocate or verbally articulate for economical reparation on its own. Rather my argument is forcefully put forward in this thesis that reparation should be for the following reasons and categories: To build permanent infrastructures in hospitals, roads, industrial projects, schools, colleges, Universities, research facilities, nuclear-power stations, technological support and scientific exchanges. These are some of the main areas and regions for economic and political empowerment. Thus European, British and American reparation would be morally, theologically, sociologically, economically and psychologically justified in beginning the long process for the restoration of Africa. But to give consistent redolence to the "moral right" "righteous justice" of reparation, African leaders should by stipulation not be placed with any responsibility for the financial allocations of the reparation funds. Both past and present African leaders have displayed tremendous irresponsibility's in managing their economies and especially foreign Aids. In addition they have not been effective in reaching appropriate economical deals and agreements for the ultimate good of their people. Selfishness is the driving force behind most African leaders leadership.

This is a major political, cultural and psychological problem in Africa.

The United Nations should take the logistic responsibility for not only the allocations of funds for the Reparation programme but to be responsible for the full and complete execution of the projects listed for comprehensive reparation. This is the juncture for the creation of African empowerment when the projects are completed. An International symposium of Black Academics, in International Laws, Economics, Engineering, Technology, Science, Agriculture, Maths, Liberation and Black Theology Theologians , Business Studies, Management, Sociology, Politics, Education and Civil-Engineering, Builders, Psychology and Architectures should meet for "Indaba" to begin the process of indigenization into the reparation system. It must be a symbiotic committed body of Diasporas and politically intelligent Africans not necessarily all leaders but from different professions.

Chapter 7
African Responsibilities for Reparation

Africa has never exploited any European country. Africa has been exploited, colonized, under-developed, oppressed , enslaved, and dehumanized. Africa has been divided up by Europe and Britain into 53 countries (Berlin Conference 1884-85) Africa has been raped and made ruthlessly under-developed. These pestiferous crimes has been done to Africa because of European and British Racism, economical avariciousness, and the dehumanization of Africans as chattels and properties. African humanity and dignity has been tarnished. Africa has been described as uncivilised and that the civilised European and British came in the name of religion through Christianization and Evangelization to enlighten Africans through a barbaric enslavement system linked to a culture of brutality based on infralapsarianism. The slaves had become symptom- zed through slavery by the ridged and rapid spread of the cultural semantical Christianity based on racism from Europe and Britain. African needs psychological and sociological liberation in order to make effective challenges to these endemic features and symptoms in African societies.

Britain and Europe had forgotten their relationships historically with the Dark Age. Alongside of the Dark Age is the Black Plague which came about through the heinous transatlantic slave trade conditions of the Middle Passage.

Africa has numerous legacies. The majority of legacies are imposed and created by the imposition of foreign cultures. Most of the foreign legacies are exigent for jettison socially, politically, religiously, economically, culturally and most importantly psychologically.

1) African political leaders should look carefully at the European Union Treaty signed in November 2nd 2009. The EU are constantly consolidating themselves economically, politically and technologically.

2) Africa needs to take positive economical responsibilities and effective care of its people. Africa should avoid always looking and expecting (Charity) from Europe, Britain and Americas. Charity in reality is disempowerment. Financial Aids ethically is a further enslavement and disempowerment of the people of Africa. This interpretation is now beginning to germinate and resonate among a few African leaders.

3) Africa must wake-up through political-unification and Pan-Africanism. The reiteration cannot be too strongly put for African-unification. The US, Europe and Britain are in special relationships. African leaders are not in special relationships with each other. This again is disempowerment. Unity, Solidarity and Symbiotic-ism are necessary smart- tools for empowerment. Israel has never shown any respect or obedience to the United Nations resolutions or to the USA. Britain and America has never fall short of their support for Israel. Despite the Israel's repugnant treatment of the Palestrina's and their

lands. Britain and America are political and economical palladium for Israel even at the United Nations. Israel is consistently being protected militarily by the US.

4) Africa can have states like the USA. Africa needs to echo with one voice, the voice as one nation of people. Africa has a shared experience of Slavery. Slavery should be in the consciousness of the nation. African countries must create their own inter-Continental – Common- Market.

African leaders must create inter-cultural exchanges socially, economically, educationally, scientifically and cultural psychologically.

Africa through the present African Union must seek Reparation for the rape and under-development of Africa. It must be a collective effort. It must be a collective demand. Africa must bear in mind that Britain in particular only operates at best when Britain can "Divide and Rule." The European and British are deeply aware of this culture. So Africa should be reminded that unity is strength. That the churches during the transatlantic slave trade in Africans encouraged and inculcated dis-unity among the Slaves.

The present President of the African Union raised the topic that: Africa must have political-unification. Immediately some African leaders reacted with the mannerism of Laodicea. They delineated no form or one drop of political ebullience towards the appeal for political-unification. Ghandi's philosophy is good for Africans. Ghandi said "Honest difference is a sign of progress".

There are fundamental and different cultures in Europe. They have had wars. World War 1, World War 2, and there was the 7 year war between Britain and France for colonies in Africa and the West-Indies. Britain used the 7 year war to divert the French attention and to capture the French colonies. In Europe Britain and France are in contiguous co-operation with technology, science and economic co-operation. Africa with all its historical cultural differences and heterogeneous demographical paradoxes must unite for the 21st century.

Africa must liberate itself from the sociological and psychological legacy of slavery. Recently in the Methodist Recorder on Thursday 24th September 2009 there was the caption. “Gambian Church elects Peter Stephens as President.” The Gambian Church has “autonomy” only on paper, but not cultural, indigenous and psychological. Not even administratively. The British Methodist Conference has been the transatlantic slave trade and deep colonial master- servant hold on the people psychologically. There were two indigenous Africans from Gambia and Ghana comprehensively qualified as candidates for the position as President. Yet, the Gambian Church elected an Englishman of 76 years old to be their President. The Gambian Church has no concept of cultural, theological, sociological and psychological indigenization. The Gambian people like most African people are psychologically enslaved. This is a common feature demographically and geographically across the great continent of Africa.

5) Africa must move urgently from “Improvidence and Impuissance” to “Self-Confidence.”

6) African counties collectively must mobilize an (African-Reparation Commission).

7) African-Caribbean- Reparation Commission is a must.

8) African-American Reparation Commission.

9) British African-Caribbean Commission.

10) The Black Churches Reparation Commission.

11) The African Union must encourage the building and formation of Business Delegations to foreign countries that are dissipating their inferior good on Africa. The USA, Britain, European countries, China and Japan.

Africa must take a page from the history of Britain's Migrant Children 1920-96. These children were forcefully removed from their parents, care homes and children centres to distant Australia. The Methodist Church, Anglican and Catholic Churches committed the pestiferous moral crime of exploitation of these children. The children were exploited, sexually and physically abused. They were traumatized. The Catholic Church Sexual Child Abuse 2010 revelation is nothing new in the Churches. It was prevalent during the transatlantic slave trade. In 2010 the Australian Prime Minister made a significant apology to all the people of this heinous crime era. The British Prime Minister followed immediately after the Australian Prime Minister, but with a difference. Britain will give reparation to these people. What of Africa? 500 years of brutal enslavement and the slaves were left in a state of destitution, ignorance and permanent dis-empowerment and backwardness. Still today, the Black Diasporas are not showing any resemblance of unity, self-respect, and the generousness of (charity) love. The Black race continue to be hostile, hateful, dis-ingenuous to each other. The level of dereliction among African leaders is a major social concern and problem to all the peoples of indigenous Africa. The fundamental dichotomy is with the

African leaders. The imprudentness of Africa is tremendously academic to the majority of the Diasporas because Africa is not moving forward but backward economically, technologically and politically. Poverty is universally pandemic in Africa at the same-time African leaders are living the resemblance of heaven on earth. They are dominated by a culture of immediacy and materialism.

Chapter 8
New Insights into Reparation

The transatlantic (Black African) slave trade is the largest subject for study. Its composition covers more than 500 years of brutality, dehumanisation of Africans, Africans as racially inferior and stultified by Europeans, British and Americans churches, philosophers and theologians. Enslaved Africans trampled under foot, culture and religion as valueless properties for the enslavers. The Churches were conjoined at its hip with the political powers. The loss of a slave by physical brutal castigation or in the case of the Zong case for Insurance claim was conceived to be only “economic loss” expendable and replaceable. Medical slave ships and plantations doctors had no moral medical regard for the slaves apart from the economic pull for themselves and the enslavers. Equally morally repugnant was the Reverends (Ministers of Religion). They too owned slaves and had slave plantations. Helen Thomas in her innovative book on Romanticism and Slave Narratives said that” Rev’d. George Whitefield approved of black slavery, and kept slaves himself. In 1748 he with others, urged the trustees of Georgia to introduce slavery into the colony, arguing that without it, Georgia would never prosper”. In most cases church leaders were extremely brutal to their slaves. At random they would shoot to death a slave in demonstration of their power. Male missionaries were pulled into the slave trade because of the prevalence of free sex. Many were required to sign that they were capable of servicing over 20 slaves. In the environment of the church movement according to the Methodist Resolution of 1784 the sources delineation is that slavery had an omnipresence in the churches. Slavery was synamous with the missionary movement, the rapid spread of Christianity and the churches. It is to be admitted that the Methodist Church had many meetings and conferences, but Prof. David Brion Davis pointed out clearly that these conferences were deeply ineffective. Even John Wesley's letter to William Wilberforce had no impact whatsoever. Furthermore, Wilberforce never supported immediate abolition but gradual abolition and he supported child slavery in Britain and he denied women liberty.

Steven Small, Dr. Anne C. Bailey, Dr. John Thornton and Dr. David Beck Ryden and others have treated the subject of Reparation for the transatlantic (Black African) slave trade in their indagation with convictions and academic sagacity. It is rather alarming that Prof. James Walvin in his book "Black Ivory- Slavery in the British Empire" second edition said "On both sides of the Atlantic, some of the finest of recent historical scholarship has emerged from this burgeoning interest in Atlantic slavery. One consequence of this scholarship has been a growing appreciation of the role of African slavery in the shaping of the modern world. Where once, not long ago, Atlantic slavery seemed a marginal and rather specialized interest, today few serious historians would deny its broad importance. In part, of course, this is because we know so much more than we did a generation ago. But the volume of knowledge is only part of the answer. There has been a qualitative shift in historical sensibility and alertness, a growing recognition that the people of Africa played a critical role in shaping the post – Columbian development of the Americas. In the process, they also served to transform the well-being of Europe."

This acknowledgement is a recent development. Development in historical scholarship is very significant. But what about the politicians? What about Theologians? What about Sociologist? What about Economists? What about the major Churches? These must have acknowledgement and development for the establishment of justice in the action of reparation. The European and British churches must take the lead not only for their moral guilt, but principally because the churches were the major engine and piston of the transatlantic slave trade and the brutalization of Africans.

At University I looked at my history Professor curriculum covering the period 1517 to present day. I noticed there was no mention of 1) The Black Presence in England. 2) No mention of the Black contributions to the economies of Europe and Britain. 3) No mention of the Black Church or Black Religions. I asked my Professor the question. Why is there no mention or reference to black people in your curriculum? He answered with confidence and conviction. "It is not important". The Black contributions are a major legacy of the slave trade and the churches involvement in the transatlantic slave trade in Africans.

The Professor answer was central to the reiteration legacy of racism in academic subjects. As a theological student both at undergraduate level and postgraduate levels, the Subject's bibliography never had one single book written on theology or history by a black theologian or historian. This is a common situation in academic departments in Britain.

My academic contact with black scholars such as Prof. James Cone, Prof. Cornel West, Dr. Eric Wiliams, Dr. Yosef A. A., Bn-Jochannan, Prof. Gayraud S. Wilmore and C.L.R. James came about bcause of my Indagation for my Doctorate in Liberation Theology.

Anthony Tibbles in his chapter "Interpreting Transatlantic Slavery: The Role of Museums" in the book "Transatlantic Slavery Against Human Dignity" with articulation he surveyed the global spectrum of the importance of the Museum in the preservation of things of historical importance to the Transatlantic (Black African) slave trade. He made it plain that some countries spent large sums of money on Museums in recognition of the economical value of the transatlantic (Black African) slave trade. Museums all around Europe and Britain are normally for the purpose of tourism, educational for schools and colleges. But what about museums in Africa and the Caribbean? Black people educationally are not well informed of the sociological, economical, political and psychological impacts of slavery and the processes of liberation, Abolition and emancipation.

Ethnographically these museums retained replications and some originals of the transatlantic slave trade. The majority of the population might not be aware of the existence of these. Three things would be of national and international importance. 1) For the Governments to have a stipulated "International Remembrance Day for Slavery." 2) A permanent Memorial symbolising Slavery. 3) The Churches ecumenically should have a "National Remembrance Day for (Black African Slavery). These would give disempowerment a new hermeneutic and dimension. The Jews have their Memorials and Museums. The Jewish Holocaust is only just 60 years ago. It is a heinous stain on the pages of Europe historically. It is also a crime against humanity. Larry D. Crawford made a very important observation about the holocaust. For him according to the dictionary, he says "What happened to European Jews does not qualify as a holocaust because it was internal". While the Transatlantic (Black African) slave trade was a crime against Almighty God and Humanity. The transatlantic (Black African) slave trade was the fundamental fuel that served and supplied the economies of Europe, Britain and America.

The major churches were centrally involved in the enslavement and dehumanisation of Africans. They too should be involved financially in reparation to Africa. The churches should have their own National and International Remembrance Day for Slavery. Black Churches must take the lead. Most historians agreed that the churches role in the transatlantic (Black African) slave trade was of paramount importance to Europe, Britain and America economically and in the establishment of white racist hegemony. Indeed without the missionary involvement by the churches, it is impossible to envisage how the two continent's governments would have dominated slavery for such a long time says Prof. Roger Anstey asking the question. "How a system/institution so morally repugnant and horrendous could have gone on for so long?" Wherever, the churches were, Britain's hegemony was a pre-domination power, exploitation, oppression and dehumanisation of Africans. . Although Britain entered the transatlantic slave trade late, Britain became the dominant power and in control of the transatlantic slave trade. Britain controlled the Gold Cost (Elmina Castle) for 145 years; with the uncompromising support of the Anglican, Methodist, Catholic, Baptist, Moravian, Quakers and United Reformed. It is important for the readers of this thesis to know that these Church buildings are still there at Elmina Castle, symbolising their direct involvement in the exploitation, oppression, dehumanization and animalization of African men, women and children. They did all these pestiferous evil deeds by the application of psyche-distance. These churches used the theology of Infralapsarianism. Theologically they saw no incongruity between the enslavement racially of Africans and their vacuous Semantical Christianity. The Methodist Church for example claimed doctrinally and theologically racially that the (Black race) was inherently inferior to whites. The Methodist Church affirmation was based on their theological justification.

Converted slaves in the Methodist Church were taught by inculcation the Capers catechism. William Caper's catechism was approved as the official catechism among negroes by the Methodist General Conference. The principle upon which this catechism was based was the 'inferiority' of the African slave and was intended to provide a theological justification for the slaves state of bondage and servitude. Bishop Othal Hawthrone Lakey in his book The Rise of Colored Methodism, gives a brief statement showing the principle upon which Capers prepared this justifying statement:

"It is obvious that much of the instruction given must, of necessity, deal in the first principles of Christian truth; must to large extent, be adopted to an humble grade of intellect, and a limited range of knowledge; and must make its impression by constant and patient reiteration."

John Wesley's and Capers Catechism were printed in the same volume. Some of the questions and answers were:

Q. What did God make man out of?

A: The dust of the ground.

Q: What does this teach you?

A: To be humble.

Q. What is your duty to God?

A. To love him with all my heart, and soul, and strength, to so worship him and serve him.

Q. What is a servant's duty to his master and mistress?

A. To serve them with a good will heartily and not with eye-service.

Professors- David T. Shannon and Gayraud S. Wilmore concluded. "It is clear that there is a feeling of superiority and paternalism being expressed toward the slave, vestiges of which are still a part of the contemporary scene. The feeling that our expression of faith had to be judged for its adequacy in the light of the standards of whites has led to some aberrations of our selves. However, we applaud the current mood of Faith and Order which seeks to give a hearing to various traditions."

It would be reasonable to lay the claim that both the Anglican Church and Methodist Church were at the forefront of the theological justification of African slavery. The Anglican Church had called for an international (Indaba) conference to debate the theological justification of slavery. The Methodist Church doctrinally and theologically sought theological justification through the inculcation and reiteration of their catechism. The Methodist Church used the method of 'brainwashing' the slaves, especially in preaching 'hell damnation' to the slaves, and at the same-time theological exculpation of the enslavers, Planters and Merchants. The Churches, European governments and the British were linked in the transatlantic dynamic system of enslavement of African slaves. The writer of this thesis postulation is twofold. a) The Churches saw no incongruity between brutally enslaving the Africans with God's approval, a white Jesus Christ and a cultural-semantical-morally-vacuous- Christianity. b) There is no evidence in culture, doctrine, theology of Infralapsarianism of deracialization. All perceptions of Africans were based on Racism and a culture of superiority. Hence the slaves were looked upon by Europeans and British by their cultural and theological premise to be physically, sociologically and psychologically disempowered and contained by the power of paralysis and dysfunctionalism through slavery. At the heart of slavery is the psychological and sociological impact of the slave trade institution on the society and psyche of Africans.

Looking now at another approach to Reparation, reparation can be practical. Money is vitally important but there are different ways to the mountain top says Buddha (Gotoma). Technological support to Africa. Scientific exposure to Africa. Agricultural support. Medical support. Free Market internationally. The obliteration of foreign debts. Building the Infrastructure, Hospitals, Schools, Colleges, Universities, Engineering, etc .Exposure to Nuclear developments. America have given all these to the Jews in addition to their vast financial compensation by Germany and unlimited military, technological and scientific support of the USA.

Dr. Basil Davidson question in his book will help us further. “The African Slave trade”. Why all the countries that were involved in the Transatlantic (Black African) slave trade made such tremendous progress and Africa remained static? Another Dr. Davidson question of importance is “Why all the technological initiatives are always European and British?

Dr. Walter Rodney “How Europe Underdeveloped Africa” made some radical conclusions. Dr. Rodney has demonstrated how Europe and Britain consistently under-developed Africa. The major areas of under-developments are 1) They denied Africa technological exchanges or partnerships. 2) Scientific exchanges. 3) They continued their exploitation of Africa’s natural resources. 4) Their perpetuation of inequality and injustices for their goods. 5) By not offering any Reparation to Africa for 500 years of rape and their profligacy (very wicked) enslavement of Africans because of their endemic racism and greed.

The Fundamental Needs of Africa

Historians, Politicians, Sociologists and Anthropologists all have different ideas and conceptualisations of African rights. These concepts might well be from the Diaspora or from exogenous sources even with valid and good intentions. Any radical and meaningful change for Africa ultimately must come from within Africa. It must be an internal-revolution. This revolution can have solid palladium and help and support from the external Diasporas. But what are the internal-revolutions guide-lines or programmes to help in the implementation process? The following list is important for this scheme of (indagation) research and study:

Industrialisation Programme
Technological Programme
Scientific Programme
Sociological Programme
Economical Programme
Political Unification Programme
Reparation Programme
Theological Programme
Psychological Programme
Decolonization Programme
Educational Programme
Indigenization Programme
Urbanization Programme

It can be much more than mere programmatic endeavours or the philosophy of pragmatic necessity for collective Africa to create positive and effective changes. The basic and essential starting point must be the revision and reversal of the Berlin Conference of 1884-85 stipulation to truncate and to divide up African into 53 countries. Prof. Seymour Drescher in his stupendous 2009 Cambridge University Publication "Abolition. A History of Slavery and Antislavery" is correct in his elucidation. Dr. Drescher says" The first international conference on Africa met in Berlin in 1884-85. Its primary purpose was to formalize the process of determining the boundaries of domination not emancipation. With the convening of the Berlin conference, the British press noted that the terms of power had clearly shifted towards a multipolar rather than a British hegemonic context."

Collective conscious solidarity first for the political unification of Africa (Africa must Unite) and the imperious determination to jettison all the reiteration legacies of the racial transatlantic (Black African) slave trade mentality. No uni-dimentional approach should be allowed or given even an introduction. It should not for the sake of safeguarding dissipation of diversion both internally and externally. The concentration focus should ultimately come from the radical implementation of the systematic programmes outlined above for the good of all Africa and the Diasporas. At the moment Africa lacks economic vibrancy and social power. It is within the sociological and the psychological understanding of the historical impacts of slavery that real liberation and political-unification will come into fruition.

Chapter 9
Black African Memoralization

I have looked with the academic aids of Lonnie G. Bunch, Anthony Tibbles, Stephen Small, Preston King and Mary E. Modupe Kolawole at various aspects of the Transatlantic (Black African) slave trade. Each in their own way have made significant contributions to "Reparation" and the place of Museums around the world today. Nonetheless, although there is a memorial National Slavery Museum in Frederickburg in Virginia in the USA according to Dr. Anne C. Bailey the appropriate place for a National Slavery Memorial symbolizing America's acknowledgement with action would be in Washington DC directly opposite the White House which was partly built by slaves from Africa.

The major countries that were involved in the heinous and barbaric Transatlantic slave trade profligate crime against God and humanity for over 500 years. Britain for example should have a National Slavery Memorial opposite the Houses of Parliament in London. Portugal, France, the Netherlands, Germany and Spain should take the lead in Europe. These countries have achieved substantial economic developments via conquest, slavery and the exploitation of African labour. It was the free labour that fed the financial accumulation, economic expansion and created the base for the industrial Revolution and the development of capitalism according to Dr. Eric Williams thesis.

There are other aspects for Memoralization of the Transatlantic (Black African) slave trade. Most of the countries that perpetuated the slave trade, will not spontaneously set up a Memorial Slavery Symbol from the perspective of moral conscience. This does include the established churches' The churches cannot be separated from the politicians. The politicians, the Royals and Church leaders combined in the enslavement of innocent Africans racially. Steven Small claimed that the Atlantic slave trade met with the full legal and political sanction of presidents, prime ministers and the leaders of the major denominations.

Africa must through its leaders provide their own Slavery Memorials. Countries such as Angola, Bight of Benin, Congo, Bight of Biafra, Nigeria and Ghana. Patrick Manning writing on The Impact of the Slave Trade on the societies of West and Central Africa forcefully reminds us thus, "The effects of the Atlantic slave trade on African life are still visible today.". There is also the admission among scholars on the question of destruction of the Continent of Africa and its peoples. Many scholars are engaged in important disputes over both facts and interpretations of the Atlantic slave trade. Most of the debates centre on the question of how seriously African society was harmed by the Atlantic slave trade. To find the fundamental sources for measured destruction of the Continent and its people, forensic hermeneutic indagation in the following areas are imperative studies. (1) Economical; (2) Sociological; (3) Psychological; (4) Anthropological; (5) Demographical; (6) Social-Anthropology; (7) Cultural; (8) Religious-Theological, and (9) Political. These tools are fundamental to the unearthing and sources.

There is a great danger in the dissipation of time and energy on the question of how much damage the Atlantic slave trade had impacted socially, demographically, economically, politically, educationally and most importantly culturally-psychologically. Africa has not began to recover. The healing has not began. The problematic situation is that Africa has not stopped emerging from the Transatlantic slave trade. There is the continuation of under-development generally across Africa. These are facts that are pertinent for the psychological, sociological and political consciousness of the importance of a National Slavery Memorial. A Memorial Day would be a good start for Africa. Africa could unite for the erection of a National Memorial Day and Memorial sight. There are many minds that share my approach and philosophy.

Another significant Memorial of the Transatlantic (Black African) slave trade, is for the creation of an African Curriculum based on the study of the Transatlantic (Black African) slave trade in all is directions. The specific period could be the 15th- the 19th centuries. The subject could well be from O'Level to undergraduate and post-graduate degrees levels This would have a tremendous impact intellectually, sociologically and psychologically- demographically on Africa today. An eximious Academic programme would be a gigantic step in the right direction. It could also envelop a special "Scholarships."

I am convinced that black people even from England looked overseas for inspiration and encouragement, from paradigms such as Olaudah Equiano and Ottobah Cuguano, Frederick Douglas, Toussaint L'Ouverture, Harriet Jacobs to Ignatius Sancho. But not all black people are aware of these immortal paradigms. Older people had not been taught about these names and today the subject is not taught adequately in some schools. Rather frankly, the subject is not generally taught.

Quite frankly, even the teachings relating to "Jesus Christ" are basically deeply influenced by European and British Racism. Theological and Philosophical Racism. Most of the Theological and Philosophical teachings are nothing but cultural perpetuation of Racism and cultural superiority. I invite any British Theologian to prove to me their concept of a white Jesus in biblical history. There is no basis for extrication from the Quest of the Historical Jesus from European and British entrenous involvement in the transatlantic slave trade. (The Black African slave trade). It was based on evilness, mendacities (lies) and Racism.

The words Mr. Johnson who was the grandson of a slave, he was reflecting on the pains and sufferings of slavery said "people need to remember about slavery." "It pains the ancestors when we forget." Lonnie G. Bunch said that in an interview with the former President Bill Clinton on his administration. "When I asked him what was the biggest surprise he experienced it is not what you think-he said but that he was stunned by the overwhelming and negative response he received when he mentioned the possibility of the President apologising about slavery. 84% of Americans felt that slavery had little or no direct meaning for them. And 80% of white American felt that slavery was simply an African American story. A further indication of fascination is the fact that 79% of black American expressed either no interest or great embarrassment about slavery. Africans and African-Caribbean should take a Sunday from Church worship or services, put their Bible under the bed and spend the day reading carefully (Kebuka) Remembering The Middle Passage Through The Eyes Of Our Ancestors by Mwalimu K. Bomani Baruti. Monday morning will appear with each individual feeling connection. Very few sermons will leave any lasting impressions as the impression from reading this tremendous book. Especially English dead cup of tea sermons without vibrancy and relevancy in the Methodist church.

Educational awareness through training and the consciousness of the nation is the best method of memorialisation of the Transatlantic (Back African) slave trade. Many of the negativisms prevalent among African-Caribbean people in Britain today are due to a very serious lack of education in terms of Black History. African-Caribbean people are not informed. They need educational consciousness. They urgently need psychic-connection. There is a congenial psychic-disconnection endemic with African-Caribbean people. I have deliberately and consciously used the prefix word above "Congenial" because Mary E. Modupe Kolawole used the term "psychic-distance" to described the evilness and the dehumanization of Africans racially by Europeans and British alike in the name of Almighty God, European Semantical- Christianity and a white Jesus Christ. It is a very serious theological aberration for British scholars of theology to lay any academic theological claim to have the moral right to offer the Black race theological hermeneutic. The Reformation movement in Europe was not only a ecclesticital dichotomy but Africa and slavery was involved. The enslavers dismissed psychologically and spiritually any psychic-connection with the slaves as human apart from their hedonistic contacts. As Mwalimu K. Bomani Baruti in (Kebuka) reminds us that the missionaries and enslavers believed that Africans did not have the capacity to truly feel pain. The slaves were branded like horses, cows and mules.

The infibulization of the slaves on slave-ships. Their ligation brutally of the slaves with whips. The pummelization traumatic syndrome of the slaves caused by beating and unabated routinisation. These and other sufferings must be remembered. There must be memorialisation of slavery. International and National Museums are not enough for the impacts psychologically in relation to the traumatisation syndromes of slavery. In other words it is a form of traumatic neurosis. African-

Caribbean people live the reiteration of slavery and all the legacies daily.

Chapter 10
African-Caribbean Radical Engagement

We have been looking at the devastation of disempowerment of Africa as a Continent and its people. The Sociological and Psychological impacts are yet to be assessed critically through academic lens, and intellect. The place of African-Caribbean scholarship could not be more real and urgent for the 21st century. It is with this consciousness that I seek to critically examine the effects of European and British dis-empowerment of the black race through racism, racial discrimination, inequalities, Injustice, brutality, prejudice and economical strangulations. The transatlantic slave trade in Africans was a ruthless system according to Dr. Bailey created by Europeans and British for the permanent dis-empowerment of Africa and the Diasporas. But the African-Caribbean slaves survived the onslaught of oppression, Racism, disempowerment physically, spiritually and psychologically.

Most scholars today and historians, especially Caucasians have consistently played down, ignored, and dismissed the greatness of the different engagements of the slaves in the process of the abolition of slavery, emancipation, Civil Rights Movement and the liberation of African people through the colonial struggles for Independence from Britain. African-Caribbean scholarship is one possibility of full scale dissipation of the myths concerning African-Caribbean disempowerment. Paradoxically, the slave trade philosophy and agenda was the creation of sempiternal dis-empowerment of Africans-descendants. But there are diachronical corrections with diacritical canon as authority which are as follows.

The Mythology and Mendacity that Britain Abolished Slavery in1807

British scholars confidently promote and articulate the mendacity and racism that the British Abolition was due to a) the abolition movement. By the dynamo of the Quakers, William Wilberforce and Thomas Clarkson. We should note carefully that there is no mention of Rev. James Ramsey who in the first place gave the instruction to Thomas Clarkson. Dr. David Beck Ryden in his book "West Indian Slavery and British Abolition 1783-1807 has pedantically corrected the grave misunderstanding and misleading information.

Here are some significant points of Dr. Ryden. First he sighted the Lord of Mansfield ruling in (William Murray) 1772 That Stewart had no right to deport James Somerset to Jamaica. "No master ever was allowed here to take a slave (from Britain) by force to be sold abroad because he deserted from service, or for any other reasons whatever." This ruling said Ryden did not emancipate all slaves from Britain but it demonstrated that the courts did indeed eradicate slavery from British soil. This ruling led some 14,000 black Britons toward freedom. Ryden also acknowledged the functions of the Quakers, Granville Sharp, Josiah Wedgwood and Thomas Clarkson and William Wilberforce. b) It was not difficult for the London Committee to marshal irrefutable evidence against the slave trade rather than the institution of slavery. c) Evidence showed that Britain was complicit in inflicting misery on hundreds of thousands of Africans. The infibulations of the slaves was that Africans were packed tightly, like sardines, in order to maximise the return for the greedy slave merchants. d) Rev. James Ramsey was a pro-abolition polemicist. But Ramsey wrote in 1788 that the opponents of the slave trade did not seek immediate emancipation because the slaves generally were not in a state wherein full liberty would be a blessing. Like children, they must be restrained by authority, and led on to their own good. This concern for the slaves was share humiliation, dehumanization and dis-empowerment. It was not paternalism, but fundamentally evilness at the extreme because the transatlantic slave trade was "extreme racism" based on psychic-distance or rather psychological-distance.

Dr. Ryden statement of Rev. James Ramsey is worthy of full quotation." For years before Wilberforce began his efforts in Parliament, Ramsey had initiated Britain's first genuine print debate on the abolition question. His criticism of slavery had a great deal more weight than those who went before-such as Anthony Benezer, John Woodman and Granville Sharp-because he had settled in the West Indies as a vicar, served as a slave doctor, and was once the owner of house slaves". Because Ramsey was an eye witness his charges against the institution were formidable. An Enquiry to the Effects of Putting a Stop to the African Slave Trade.1784 and An Essay on the Treatment and the Conversion of African Slaves in the British Sugar Colonies.

Ramsey's position was assertive and powerful. According to Dr. Ryden Rev. Ramsey proposed to shatter the entire colonial system of slavery, replacing it with humanity, liberty, Christianity and free-labour.

According to Dr. Ryden thought-provoking book it is undeniable that Rev. James Ramsey contribution made some difference. At the same-time I have shown that Prof. James Walvin and many others have failed to see that scholarship must have rectitude and not be inundated with cultural prevarications.

Another in-accurate claim is that Britain Abolition of Slavery was on moral grounds. Britain had no Moralization on the slave trade. Britain had always been a pagan nation. Christianity was only Cultural Semanticalism. Moralization was the argument of the Enlightenment. The Enlightenment was only a jejune period of intellectualism. It had no other credence. Nothing based on moralization and theologization. Theo-centrically according to British scholars such as Prof. Roger Anstey and James Walvin played down the force of Dr. Eric Williams' argument (Capitalism and Slavery): abolition became possible because slavery had become un-economical. Prof. Walvin on the other-hand claimed that Britain abolished the slave trade because Britain felt that she had a divine mission to do so. This is utter rubbish. The chronological reality was that Britain and America continued the slave trade up to 1888 in Brazil and some modern scholars are now stating strongly that the slave trade continued up to the 1920's and beyond. The author of this present thesis shares this modern concept and argument. James Walvin only point of common-sense is what he said "The mythology of abolition lived on to become part of the accepted canon of British historiography." Prof. Walvin has integrated the jejune claim of Prof. Roger Anstey's claim that the brutal enslavement of Africans was part of God's Salvation History which he obtained from Prof. Hans Conzelmann 'delayed parousia' is synonymous with Salvation History.

Slaves Radical Engagements

There are some significant dates relating to slave revolts and abolition of the transatlantic slave trade in Africans that we should note with appreciation. Vicissitudes created by the slaves on large estates in Jamaica begun to unsettle the imposition of slavery and social order of slave colonies. The "Tacky's Revolt" in 1760-61 when 400 slaves rebelled in St Marys's Parish on the north coast of Jamaica, an uprising which dramatically resulted in the execution of 400 suspected slave rebels and the precipitous deportation of 500 others to British colonies. Other significant slave insurrections included Gabriel Prossere's revolt in Virginia; 1800.Bussa's rebellion in Barbados in 1816, Denmark Vesey's revolt in South Carolina in 1822, the slave rebellion in Demerara 1823 and Nat Turner's revolt in Virginia 1831. These chronologies juxtaposed to these revolts made the abolitionist campaigns equally important. The period 1788, 1792 and 1814 was against the slave trade; 1823,1830 and 1833 was against slavery; 1838 was principally against the "apprenticeship" of former slaves.

Dr. Richard Hart in his Vols. 1&2 of Slaves Who Abolished Slavery argued forcefully that the slave revolutions contributed powerfully to the abolition of the heinous crime of slavery. Walvin mentioned historically correctly the Haitian revolution which American feared could become contagious and warned Britain of this great danger; the great rebellion in Barbados in 1816, in Demerara in 1823 and in Jamaica in 1831-32. These were mighty rebellions and because of their potential power aggregate and in solidarity British attitude and outlook was deeply divided. It was the slaves' audacity and ontological gift inherently inspired them and they in return dictated the chronology for the abolition of slavery. Nothing to do with the vacuous claimed made by Britain for humanitarian, moral grounds, dissident radical Protestantism or radical evangelistical social conscience. Dr. Moses D. E. Nwulia argued that Britain had no dominating interest in the 19th century towards the eradication of slavery or the regeneration of Africa. If there were any grain of truth in their claim, it was for humanitarianism self-interest and nothing moral. But for the value of information the delegalization of slavery was based on the Ghandi model which Britain used reluctantly. Dr. Nwulia further elucidated the claim of abolition by assuring us that it was the 'legal status of slavery but not slavery.'

Chapter 11
The Churches and Semantical –Cultural –Christianity

The Churches were powerful palladium for the British impressive hold on the Transatlantic (Black African) slave trade .The Churches function was the evangelization and Christianization of the African people. Walvin writing in Transatlantic Slavery Against Human Dignity claimed that the Non-conformists in Britain were outraged to hear the stories about the punishments inflicted on their black co-religionists. In the Caribbean inlands the black Christianity produced its own changes. 1) The new chapels provided the slaves with a meeting place away from the plantation. 2) The chapels offered the powerful black preachers, steeped in the imagery and vocabulary of the Bible. The O.T. was replete with imagery and relevance for the slaves who were in bondage awaiting for salvation and freedom. 3) Black Christianity impressed white visitors with their noise and enthusiasm. 4) Black church leaders demanded a salvation existentially in the here-and-now.

This is generally Walvin thesis. However, Christianity was basically an outlet but not a vehicle for liberation from oppression. The slaves looked not to Christianity which was oppressing them. But to their African religion namely Myalism. Christianity was a reminder and symbolism of oppression. The Moravian Church fought with Myalism for 100years in Jamaica and the same period in the USA. Walvin goes on to say that Britain Abolished Slavery first in 1807, then in 1834 and finally in 1838. Walvin ascribed all these to Britain. Walvin is comprehensively wrong. It was the dynamism of the slaves revolutions that dictated the time- table for abolition not the British. It was the slaves resilience and determination to jettison slavery having been moved beyond vocabulary by the inner spirit of Myalism and the hand of God. The slaves were engaged in their own liberation. In Haiti the dynamic revolution leader Toussaint L'Ouverture beat the French, Spanish and the British.

Prof. Walvin dates of 1834 and 1838 were times of the slaves revolution for emancipation not Chattel slavery. Their immortalized names are. Nanny of the Windward Maroons, Cudjoe, Tacky, Nat Turner, (USA) Sam Sharpe, Paul Bogle, Stephen Small and James Walvin have stated that 'Free Blacks were active not only within their own nations, but also in establishing international links.' Africans throughout the Diaspora travelled to oppose slavery and the oppression and exploitation of Africans. From the United States, activists and educators such as Martin Delany, Edward Wilmott Blydon. Sarah Remond Parker Phillis Wheately and Alexander Crummel travelled to England across Europe. In the eighteen century Britain, the works of Ottobah Cuano, Estaban Montejo, Olaudah Equiano and Ignatius Sancho challenged slavery and the vilification of Africans. M .L. King, Frederick Douglas, The Black Panthers, W.E.B.Du Bois. Angela Davis, Malcolm X. Mary Secole, Queen Mother Moore, Mama Africa. Miriam Makeba, Harriet Tubman, Corretta King, Anna Murray, and beyond the period of slavery, emancipation to the struggles against discrimination, inequality, Civil

Rights and Injustice. These are some of the immortal black revolutionary leaders who gave their lives for freedom and liberation of African-descendants from the yokes and bondage of the transatlantic slave trade which was based on racial difference and Racism.

Historiographical Literature

The historiographical literature is abundant with diacritical evidence of blacks physical engagement in the action of revolution and liberation. Thanks must be given to the erudite C L. R. James for his book "The Black Jacobins. Here James outlined for us with shining articulation the engagement of Toussaint L'Ouverture and the San Domingo Revolution of tremendous engagement in warfare. These were black engagements, reclaiming their empowerment psychologically, physically and spiritually. Walvin had overlooked that contiguous relationship between the transatlantic (Black African) slave trade and Christianity- British which was semantical cultural Christianity. That the enslavement of Africans was committed in the name of Almighty God, British Christianity and Jesus Christ.

The slaves were forcefully disempowered by the extreme act of racism and deep psychological disconnection between slaves and enslavers. The loss of empowerment as a human being was because of the excessive and brutal dis-regard for black humanity and the effectuation of the traumas suffered by the slaves ranging from post-traumatic slave syndrome, through the historical trauma into the trauma of stultification traumatic syndrome. In all areas and dimension of disempowerment, engagement, memorialisation and historical museums. My hope and theory of Educational Academic memorialisation through the Transatlantic (Black African) Slave Trade as a major subject of National and International importance. We must remember not that we were sold, but that we were strong. And we must not remember that we were kidnapped, but that we were resilient and audacious. Slavery was theologically, sociologically, politically and economically very apocalyptic for the slaves but they reclaimed their rightful empowerment and engagement for liberation.

"Immortal words of men who re-claimed their empowerment and contextual engagement."

M. L. King: "I have held many things in my hands, and have lost them all; but whatever I have placed in God's hands, that I still possess."

Nelson Mandela: "As we are liberated from our fear, our presence automatically liberates others."

Bob Marley: "In this bright future you can't forget your past."

President Barack Obama: "America, this is your moment. This is our time. Our time to turn the page of the policies of the past."

Malcolm X: "A man who stands for nothing will fall for anything."

These quotations are for inspiration, encouragement and hope. They are prophetic and full of soteriological message for our age.

Chapter 12
Black African Women Disempowerment and Assiduous Engagement

Black women had been sexually- abused, sodomized, dehumanised, disrespected and discriminated against throughout the transatlantic slave trade history. Achievements and contributions in history are looked up-on to be by men. We sometime forget the biblical maxim that God created all humans as equals with the divine endowment of freedom and liberty. . However, human society and human beings does not function just like that. Even with the philosophy of Marxism, the process leading economically to an ultimate classless society is fanciful, mythological and deeply economically chimerical. I shall demonstrate in this chapter some of the historical and significant periods and situations that belong specifically to black women. These situations are times when black women re-claimed their empowerment and their engagement in the process of history, abolition, manumission and emancipation.

Biblically the mighty liberation of God's oppressed people in Egypt from oppression is ascribed to Moses and Aaron leadership. To Moses his political, psychological and religious ability to have expostulated the mind of Pharaoh and at the same-time inculcated into the slaves whose total mental orientation was slave-based their aggregate empowerment. That the slaves themselves had the potential to liberate themselves. This is to do with psychological consciousness. Humankind was created with the ontological gift of free-will, freedom and liberty. The potential consciousness for liberty is essentially a theological gift from God.

Women played a major part in the liberation and Exodus movement which was principally political, human, economical and according to the biblical editors deeply religious in that God revealed divine power (I am avoiding using "Him") through the powerful cosmic mind and energy the will for the oppressed children to be free. The women cared for the men and children. The significance of women is dramatically played out in the invasion of the Promised Land.

The Exodus experience became a biblical, historical and theological paradigm for the oppressed people and indeed according to liberation theology, it is a paradigm for the exploited, down-trodden, the powerless, the voiceless and the oppressed. What is most remarkable in the Exodus movement and experience was the programme and strategy to enter the Promised Land. The biblical narratives are fascinating and powerful. But what is of historical importance and the paradigmatic model is that it was the women who planned the actual entry. It was the women who took the audacious lead how to enter into the Promised Land. The women were the front line soldiers.

Jumping the queue of time and thinking to the ministry of Jesus, women played a major theological role in Jesus' ministry. Women that were the outcast like the untouchables in society. Mary the great prostitute became Jesus most trusted disciple and major personality in the early church. Jesus gave to the disposed liberation, restoration, empowerment and engagement in society. At the crucifixion of Jesus we are told by the Evangelists, that the men fled and abandoned Jesus just at the moment when Jesus needed their support, help and solidarity. The women remained assiduous to Jesus especially at his challenging moment of crisis, alienation and estrangement. The women were there. And at Jesus Resurrection it was the women who experienced the Risen Christ first. It was the women who received the Good News. It was the women who carried the Good News. "He is risen from the dead". Women are prodigious creatures throughout history.

Mary E. Modupe Kolawole writing on "An African View of Transatlantic Slavery and the Role of Oral Testimony in Creating a New Legacy. Her academic articulation and contribution relates to the following pertinent arguments.

1) She began with a decisive statement. Some important decision that were to affect Africa's very existence were taken without consulting the Africans. In 1494, the Treaty of Tordesillas, a precursor of the Berlin conference of 1884, shared out the world between Spain and Portugal, allocating Africa to Portugal.

2) The moral implication of the racially constructed transatlantic slave trade, and it's obvious contradiction of Christian teachings and ideals. Doctrinal and theological ambiguities.

3) Some writers still try to validate transatlantic slavery to alleviate the sense of guilt. Many Western writers nonetheless document it with

scholarly sincerity and integrity. It is however, generally accepted that African slaves formed the backbone of European economic enrichment in the Caribbean colonies and contributed directly and indirectly to European economic and industrial growth.

4) After African labour become indispensable and this accounts for the duration and continuous attraction of the transatlantic slave trade in African slavery. Inevitably, the transatlantic slave trade created an African Diaspora in Europe and Americas. The consequences, in the creation of a new legacy and new racist ideologies are ubiquitous, shaping several aspects of the lives of Africans. Europeans and Americans. Many people believe that the wealth of cities such as Liverpool is inextricably linked to the transatlantic slave trade.

5) Africans, however, attempt to revisit history through anthropological, archaeological, oral literary, oral historical and diverse other sources to objectify the existence and portray the transatlantic slave trade from the horse's mouth. To the African, the devastation suffered physically, psychologically, emotionally and morally almost defies atonement. Indeed, some of the socio-political problems that are peculiar to blacks in the Diaspora today take root in a scene of an omnipresent past and historical justice. Domestic slavery was not racially constructed, nor did it involve the repugnant scope of degradation, geographical dislocation, cultural disorientation or forced acclimatization and attendant devastation and death.

Chapter 13
African Women's peculiar degradation in Transatlantic slavery

I have explained the nature and function of baracoon and the creation of (Barracoonization Traumatic Syndromes). Young women of breeding age were placed equally with robust young men purely for breeding. They were like animals breeding to supply and multiply the slave masters stocks. The brutal treatment of the women are listed and described fully in my book The Psychological Combination of Christianity and Slavery, The impact on African-Caribbean Psyche.

African men in slavery were abused by the following means: physically, brutally degraded, dehumanized, sodomized and animalized, robbed of their manhood and humanity, dignity, freedom and power. African men were psychologically and spiritually destroyed. African men were forced to watched their wives, daughters and mothers being raped by white men publicly.

The power was with the slave master. A male slave wife or girlfriend was not his personal person or partner. The slave master had all rights and first choice over the woman. The women, be they wife or girlfriend were sexed openly on the plantations in full view of all the slaves. Thereby it was an act and demonstration of ownership, domination and omnipotent power over the minds of all the slaves. Slaves were stripped of all human characteristics and dignity. The fundamental function of the evil system of slavery was that the conditions and treatment of the slaves on the plantations was equal to that of horses, cows and goats.

Women were severely punished for ignoring the attempts of the masters' sexual advances. Sometimes women were killed, or hanged on a tree limb for the crows. Some had parts of the body amputated for refusing sexual desires of the masters. Slave women had no choice. They had no freedom. They were expected to respond immediately to the call of the master's sexual whim. Physical, emotional and psychological survival of Black women in these conditions and environment is a tremendous demonstration of the gigantic strength of Black women.

Kolawole writing on the degradation of African women in the transatlantic slavery reminds us of the fundamental difference to that of traditional African domestic slavery. Women slaves in the African tradition or context were often domestic hands to the rich and as a result they enjoyed a better condition of life than most women. However, this was not unique to Africa. The same terms and conditions existed in the USA and the Caribbean region. In Africa, women leaders such as Madam Tinubu of Abeokuta and Lagos and Queen Amina of Zaaria had many female slaves.

The transatlantic (Black African) slave trade institution was of a different character and function to traditional African slave society. Emphatically, the transatlantic slave system brought an indescribable level of agony and unprecedented quest for enslavement. It was because of the strong desire for African goods according to Dr. Walter Rodney. Goods like alcohol, tobacco, firearms, chamber pots, guns and clothes. According to Dr. Walter Rodney, European and British goods were inherently inferior, and in the main goods that European and British rejected. In conjunction with this type of measure and condition, youthful men and girls were forcefully extracted and uprooted from their demographical roots, customs, traditions, family, neighbours and friends. Two powerful forces were at work here. First, the excortication relating to human qualities of all slaves. Whatever, characteristics pertaining to Africanism, these were radically stripped, even names. In other words a new identity was given. That identity was of the slave master. Nothing, absolutely nothing resembling African history, traditions and customs was allowed. Second, the deracination of all the people. It was not a matter of negotiation or reciprocal arrangements. The slaves were dramatically and forcefully uprooted. The combination of excortication and deracination created two of the most devastating post traumatic slave syndromes for the African men and women slaves. With the constant permeation of these slave syndromes there is to this day the perennial daily reiteration traumatic slave syndromes legacy. It was physical and psychological dehumanization traumatic syndrome. Degradation and suffering had no limitation for the women. The intensification attraction of European goods made African leaders more rapacious to acquire slaves for the slave markets. The European and British inundated the African communities with firearms which intensified inter-tribal wars. The brutality of the situation, made Africans more hardened and the women were made into steel of hardness and courage. With the women there were internal resistance. Men taken into slavery created tremendous shortage of men, while the women were in abundance for the edacity of the men left behind. The men found the rapid cultivation of the availability of women conducive and many married several wives.

A prolific observation of Mary E. Modupe Kolawole is germane for this thesis. We can only estimate the physical and psychological degradation with the dehumanization of women and children. I began this section with the audacity and contribution of women. Kolawole observation is that the transatlantic slave trade brought new levels of degradation and suffering to African women. Men married more wives to produced more children, this was a reliable source for the slave market.

Kolawole says "Between 1724 and 1727, King Agaja of the providence of Mahoney sold large numbers of female slaves before the loss of Ouidah terminated his trade. The significance of motherhood and mothering for African women is tremendously prodigious. Its within this sphere of profound humanity, compassion and emotion African motherhood is to be located and contextualized. The intensity and agony during this nadir of human degradation says Kolawole. Women experienced the ultimate violation of their dignity and the truncation of their self-esteem during slavery, including the Middle Passage and its continuation till the post-bellum period of the African Diaspora. Dr. Joy Leary in her book Post-Traumatic Slave Syndrome tried to capture this moment of African women's history when she told the story of her first visit to Africa. A good area to begin the long and deep process of understanding the transatlantic slave trade period is the commencement with women and children Dr. Leary says.

For some historians, sociologists and anthropologists, African Women during the Atlantic (Black African) slave trade accepted enslavement, subjugation and dehumanization as their karma without any measure of recalcitrance. This impression, elucidation and information from white scholars is not correct. Historically there are histographic literatures and documents that substantially delineates the story and journey of how African women resisted slavery. Slave Narratives written by African women was a powerful weapon against the slave trade and the abolition movement to abolish slavery and the abolishment of slavery. Nanny the Maroon of the Windward Maroons in 1733. The Jamaican Rebellions of 1834 and 1838. The Morant Bay Rebellion in St. Thomas in the East led by Paul Bogle. 1865. Sam Shape in 1831 Christmas Rebellion. The Baptist Revolution.

Gad Heuman in his book a Warwick University Caribbean Studies contribution "The Killing Time" "The Morant Bay Rebellion in Jamaica." Said the rebellion showed the maturity of the slaves in formulating a rebellion against political slavery. He continued that the Haitian Revolution and the rebellion of 1831 serve as paradigms of protest against slavery. The Tacky rebellion in 1760 is seen as another good example. But the example is the acknowledgement and demonstration that women played a tremendous functional role in these rebellions. At Sandy Gully when the men were having trepidation and about to change their minds, it was the women who encouraged the men to press on. At times the women took the lead.

We have to depend on the fragmented histographical literature and records to validate the importance of the experience of slavery, the resistance of the slaves and the slaves resilience and preservation. Biblically and theologically the disciples of Jesus and the early Christians of the Jesus Movement were oppressed, frightened and persecuted. The ingredients for their endurance was the oral tradition or oral transmission method they used. The slaves used the effective tool of resistance and resilience to transcend their traumatic syndrome created by slavery. Their resilience was grounded in the power of oral poetry and folk-tales. The disciples wrote down and told stories about Jesus which became a tradition. (Form Criticism and Redaction Criticism) N.T. scholars have used these tools to understand more about the Jesus Movement. Dr. Norman Perry and Dr. E.P. Saunders have relied on these methods.

Laudation of African women, during the transatlantic slave trade period is full of fascination and love. Sometimes Delphic but intriguing. The African women focus primarily on the indescribable and irreparable damage and trauma caused by the barbaric and peculiar psychic interaction of the community living in slave society. There is no terminus to the reiteration of the transatlantic (Black African) slave trade legacies. These legacies are determined centrally on racism as legacy discrimination, prevalent poverty, powerlessness, suboptimization traumatic syndrome still persisting today. But we see the women in their reclaimed power and contextualization of engagement and in re-engagement they are finding liberation, empowerment, their dignity and their womanhood and children being restored.

Chapter 14

African-Caribbean Self-Disempowerment and Dis-engagement

It is well established that the transatlantic slave trade Africans has created havoc on the continent of Africa. The devastations are demographical, political, economical, cultural, sociological and psychological. It does include also the Caribbean region and most of the African Diaspora. It is further diacritical in the deleterious realms of poverty, under-development and dis-empowerment that the evidence and traumatic syndromes are very prevalent among African descendants. Psychologically and culturally many see themselves more British thank having much African identity and history connections. We can also without any academic energy tabulate the sources and evidence of injustice, racism and inequality in relation to African-Caribbean people or community.

The transatlantic (Black African) slave trade is one powerful and historical existential and historical experience in point. The fundamental need to know the past and to be better equipped to determine better the present and then the future is not a major priority for the vast number of African-Caribbean community. At the same-time African-Caribbean people are normally or appear to be normally extremely pre-occupied with their lives in seeking to emulate European and British cultures rather than the African connection and consciousness. That is their existential and empirical lives conditioned by the transatlantic slave trade philosophy of powerlessness. What are the pre-eminent pre-occupations? What are the immediate challenge or challenges? According to Dr. Richard Hart, African-Caribbean people are looked upon as the door-mats of society? This is generally so sociologically, economically, culturally and particularly politically. Dr. James Cone writing from the African-American context said, that the peoples of the world with dark skin are in the main the poor and dispossessed in the world. The writer of this thesis main postulation and passionate belief and observation is that the reiteration legacies of the transatlantic slave trade is strongly evident in the permanent dis-empowerment of the Black race. Why is there so much stagnations within the African-Caribbean community? Why are there so much complacency among the African-Caribbean community? Why are there no real visible cohesive symbiotic social groups of African-Caribbean for radical changes coming from the African-Caribbean community? All these questions and critiques are directly connected to the legacies of the transatlantic (African-Caribbean) slave trade. Unless, there is a tremendous collective- consciousness-psychic-connection with African-Caribbean community, first educationally re: the combined history of African-Caribbean as absolutely imperative and urgent. Second- inter-connectional trust, confidence, respect and the authentic sense of belonging as a people with a shared past that connect all African-Caribbean people. That past is the transatlantic (Black African) slave trade. Anthropologically the transatlantic (Black

African) slave trade is the in- destructible emotional, spiritual, physical, cultural, political, economical and psychological connections of Africa and the Diasporas.

Where do we go from here? What are the aims and objectives? Is there an Agenda?

It is necessary to know where we are coming from first. The Middle Passage in terms of kebukka is the fundamental alpha of the journey and story. The educational structures and curriculum for schools are designed to alienate and impede authentic development of African-Caribbean children and African children. Black comprehensive history is not imperative for the curriculum. In a recent conversation with my 15 year old daughter about her educational development and her consciousness of her historical past and the slave trade. She said, all that she knew is what I talked about at home. Nothing in her school curriculum deals with constructive and positive black history. Black history, the transatlantic slave trade is not systematically taught in secondary schools. It is at the appropriate age of Primary and Secondary Education that African-Caribbean descendants children should be learning with pride their rich past. It is key for them to see African-Caribbean role models and paradigms in their school. The former Boxing World Champion Mike Tyson said in November 2009 on a British TV, interview. "That he himself had not thought of becoming President of the United States of America. But that his eleven year old son, now frequently said to him, dad I would like to become like President Barack Obama." What his son is now seeing which he had not and could not have seen was "The possibility". He now knows that "Yes you Can."

There is a common habit and tradition for people to castigate the systems. The past. The pains, sufferings and rejections that comes with the reiteration legacies of the transatlantic slave trade combined with physical, psychological, spiritual and demographical consciousness of psychic-connection. There are valid reasons and grounds for this type of castigations. But how do we deal with these major challenges, hurdles and mountains? The immediate problem is that individuals are ineffective, modicum groups are trying to do some things. The building of a wasp nest, or beehive is done by every member working together for the collective body. I once watched a pack of Lions on the National Geographical Programme. They were starving for a very long time. Every hunt was a failure. The two male lions were away for weeks perambulating their area. Out of desperation two female lions made the voluminous sound which was interpreted by the reporter that they were crying to their male leaders for help, protection and provision. The male lions responded. It was marvellous to watch how the two male lions co-ordinated their hunts. Every member was in position properly. There were the chasers. The co-ordinators and the catchers. Their first hunt was successful and all fed all night. African-Caribbean people can learn how to co-operate. How to unite for the same goals. African-Caribbean people's amelioration needs cultivation.

It is a painful existential-empirical experience and observation that African-Caribbean people are the major architect of their own failures. There is abundant evidence that African-Caribbean people create their own dis-empowerment and dis-engagements. The sleeping giant of African-Caribbean people is coming together. 'To unite'. One such powerful example is the Black-led-Churches in Britain. These are full of competitors and negative competitions. Yes, there are reciprocal visits and exchanges but coming together as a Social Voice. A Political Voice. As an economic Force is a foreign concept and culture. These are not even epistemological visions or dreams, they are historical reiteration legacies. The thought is just not there. The thought of Liberation Theology is not there. Black Theology is not there. But, paradoxically, the belief and singing, of "When I get to heaven, I am going to put on me shoes and dance all over heaven" is very common on Sundays.

It was existential for the slaves says Dr. James Cone to sign like that. Most of the negro spiritual songs are highly existential. They are also highly situational. The transatlantic legacies are tangling the necks of the young and shortly the adults will give up the ghost because the biological clock says so. Despair, exhaustion and bewilderment are prevalent in the African- Caribbean community. Where is the prophetical voice to say "nil desperandum." The transatlantic (Black African) slaves knew how not to accommodate despair. They had the spirit and courage of obdurability. They were very precocious slaves. They knew that the sun that rises will also sets on them. And tomorrow it will rise again. They kept entrenous in their hearts and lives the fire of Myalism. It was that fire that touched the life of Nat Turner, David Brown, Frederick Douglas, Harriett Jacobs, Phillis Wheately and Toussaint L'Ouverture. It was the same fire that touched Tacky in 1760 and Sam Sharpe and Paul Bogle. In 1834 and 1838. The same fire ignited again in 1865 with the struggle for emancipation because of the dynamic power of the inner nil desperandum . (Quobna Ottoban Eugoano) he was the first African slave to demand total abolition of all slaves, and the slave trade.

Marcus Garvey, M.L. King, Malcolm X and countless others male and female they all grasped the fire that Moses kept his eyes on. To end the journey is good and the ultimate goal. But to be part of that journey is encapsulating, powerful and consummating. To be part of change. To see change. To know that you too were instrumental in that change.

Jesus Commissioned his 12 disciples in Matthew chapter 1O. “And as ye go, preach saying, The kingdom of heaven is at hand. Heal the sick, cleanse the lepers, raise the dead, cast out devils, freely ye have received freely give.” African-Caribbean people mission is gigantic. One cannot be effective singularly. Coming together as a people can be effective. A Pan- African people with one aim, one goal and one destiny. Separation is not only weakness but it is disempowerment and dis-engagement, it is destruction. God’s Kingdom is wholeness. It is total Shalom. The Black race is not only a deeply fractured race of people because of the impact of 500 years of brutal slavery but principally the Black race lacks Shalom. This is basically intactness. It is the dynamic kenosis. It is liberation. It is ‘Kebuka’ remembering the ancestors, their spirits are still crying, their groans are emical sounding, they are restless because their off -springs continue with the transatlantic slave trade reiteration legacies. The combined consciousness, the psychic-connection has become for African-descendants more than a epistemological dream but an eschatological hope linked to salvation. The slaves were stripped or excoriated of all human sense of freedom, justice, liberty, equality and manumission. It is the right of all African-Caribbean descendants to re-claim the rights of self-esteem, respect, personhood and the right as a child of God, made in the divine image of God with the potential to become like God through the Black Jesus of the Black experience.

Chapter 15
The Transatlantic Slavery Story

There are different synonymous terminologies that are being used frequently by historians to specifically identify the period of the most horrendous crime ever committed by man against God and Humanity. 1) The Transatlantic (Black African) Slave Trade. 2) The Middle Passage. 3) The Atlantic slave trade. 4) The Triangular Circle. 5) The Slave Trade. 6) The African Holocaust. Which-ever terminology is used for convenience the annotation is the same story. Stories are powerful reports, memories, accounts of events, messages, authentic narratives, allegories, parables and pericopes. Outside of a number of biblical accounts such as the Exodus Story, The Crossing of the Reed Sea, Jonah and the Whale, Daniel in the Lions Den, Jesus Walking on the Water, the Virgin Birth, the Resurrection of Jesus and the Transfiguration, to mention only a few. The greatest story is the survival of Africans in the most horrific and flagitious human enslavement for 500 years. According to Dr. Vincent Harding in his book "There is a River. The Black Struggle for Freedom in America," he claimed that over 100,000,000 African slaves died in the Middle Passage crossing (One hundred million died in the Atlantic Crossing). Enslavement by

Europeans, British and Americans. People who claimed that they were civilised. They claimed that they were Christians. They developed their Missionary Societies. They built Churches and Missions. They set their Communion Table above the largest dungeon with 1000 men, women and children imprisoned not for any anti-social conduct, robbery or evil needs, but because of their race and black skin. The crime was indeed the immoral crime of the British, European and Americans was their "White Racism" David Fleming said "This is a story which must be told, and we must not heed those who believe it should be consigned to the history books. The legacy of this horrendous slave trade lives on, in racism and intolerance, in the plight of Africa and many other people of African descent, and in the rich cultures of Africa, African-Caribbean, African-American and African-European people."

The greatest "Story is the Transatlantic (Black African) slave trade story." Its story must be told with the extrication of abashment. People who are abashed cannot tell this story. They cannot write this story; only those with a deep, deep psychic-connection, spiritual-connection, cultural-connection. Historical connection and psychological-connection and collective-connection can authentically articulate this phenomenological, historical and theological story. It is a story about the dehumanization and animalization of Africans. The brutal deracination of Africans to fuel the European and British economies with free labour and their rapacity of economic greed and a culture of perceived -superiority. It is a story of the aberration of British, European, and Americans from any moral, social, ethical and theological connection with decency. This story must be told. It has to be told. There can be no healing until the story is told and understood loud and clear. The story must end with restitution and reparation for 500 years of blatant wrongs. Political Unification is a must for Africa. The Slaves Narratives is a must for reading in the homes, among the Black families in Schools, Colleges and Universities.

David Fleming asked the pertinent question. Why such an inhuman trade could be conducted by a supposedly civilized Western culture over such a long period? Dr. Roger Anstey asked a similar question. How a trade so morally horrendous and repugnant could have continued for so long? The answers hopefully will be found in the stories themselves. The ancestors' spirits, the women's voices and stories, the voiceless children and the men who were reduced to powerless beast of burden and cattle.

It is the story of descriptive sexual abuse of the slaves in the form of beastliness and sodomization. The slaves were robbed of the human dignity, robbed of emotions and passions when an infant was taken from his/her mother. The slaves were robbed racially because of racism, trampled-underfoot by heartless pagans because they were Africans.

Culturally and religiously flagitious British people. African slaves valued only by a number, without worth, only the worth of a chattel, the only meaning is work, work from morning to night. The slaves were considered to be fit only for breeding on the plantations like rabbits, pigs, goats, dogs, horses and mules for the economic prosperity of the enslavers. To provide wealth for their mansions in England. The famous Great House in Dunson Park in Bexleyheath in Kent is a powerful example. Defined by pagans whites, and classified by the Jesus of the African experience as white tombs, void and soulless, sin-filled with bitterness, hate, selfishness and avariciousness, for all is vanity says the Wise man of Wisdom of old Solomon.. It comes and goes at a flash of the lightening. What is man that he flourishes in the morning dew and disappears with the evening sun. As Dr. Anne E. Bailey puts it "The image of the rows and rows of African in the hold of the ships, without room at their heads and with their feet piled on one another, was to become one of the most powerful antislavery images. The image, which leaves few details to the imagination."

It is the story of the 'Kebuka.' 'Middle Passage' and 'Maafa' The Great Destruction journey of the Atlantic slave trade in physical terms-shackles, large numbers of African slaves packed like sardines in too-small holds; air thick with the smell of urine, blood, and tears: and the dead strewn in the midst of the living.

The Ghanaian writer and activist Casely Hayford commenting in a stinging critique on Missionaries in Ghana and the Missionary presence in Sekondi said. "And this the sum total of a half a century of missionary zeal and effort. Could it be for this that the simple good hearted fathers of our races had suffered and died. They prayed for light themselves and for their children's children. But instead of light, say ye God, does not darkness brood over the land?"

The oral stories needs an audience to tell their stories, the Gospels are stories of Jesus. The Transatlantic slave trade story, is the story of Africa and her sons and daughters. The oral stores like the Gospels must be written down in exoterical languages unblemished by lies, but the inscription like that on the Cross, the ink of the slaves in the dungeon and slave ships, must be the slaves tears, blood, urine, death and the rest of human physical dissipation, even sweat. These stories must be inscribed in our memories. We the Black race will not tell that we were sold but we shall tell the story that they were brave, resilient, procacious and strong. Strong not by physical strength, but by the will and spirit. They had survived the pain, suffering, whippings, dehumanization, subjudication and slaughter? Charles Wesley the Hymn writer expressed in inner emotions "Help us to help each other Lord. Each others cross to bear, Let each his friendly aid afford. And feel his brother's care." In African Diaspora throughout the world runs in their veins the blood of those mighty men and women from the barracoons and plantations. Those who were bound by chains and yokes far away. Dis-empowered, raped of their dignity. The dungeons, slave ships and Middle Passage. The engagement of listening and reading the stories of the African past. The past is now the reiteration legacies we live by, not by geo-social distance but by the physic-bond and connection of the transatlantic slave trade. The traumatic syndromes of the transatlantic slave trade are indeed part of the reiteration legacies process today in the continuation impact of slavery.

African- Caribbean descendants who are abashed by the transatlantic (Black African) slave trade institution and history do so out of psychic-disconnection or psychological disconnection and intellectual ignorance. Another legacy is need for cultural and spiritual collective consciousness-connection. This legacy warrants with urgency the need for a National and International Curriculum based on the Transatlantic (Black African) slave trade covering 500 years of slavery in Africans. In addition, the creation of An International Symposium of Historians and academics including Liberation Theologians coming symbiotically as intellectuals for the implementation of a radical Black central Curriculum. This too would be a solid memorialisation of the transatlantic slave trade for generations to come. The Black churches should be involved also, seeing that the Black churches has no psychic-connection with the heinous-flagitious transatlantic slave trade in Africans and it was basically the White churches psychic-distance morally why they continued the heinous transatlantic slave trade in Africans for so long. Prof. Roger

Anstey posed the question. Why the immoral transatlantic slave trade in Africans was allowed to continued for so long? It was the slaves revolts and rebellions that dictated the diary for abolition. It had nothing to do with as claimed by white scholars of a British Moral conscience. Or self-interest. 0r Evangelistically movement and Intellectualism Movement. Not even the claimed Dissident Protestantism.

Chapter 16
Prodigious Male and Female Slaves Resistance

Transatlantic (Black African) slave trade was a facinorous system and institution programmatically designed to redefine and re-categorized Africans into a permanent state of dis-empowerment, powerlessness, dysfunctionalism and paralysis. The powerlessness envisaged by the Enslavers, Merchants, Governments, Presidents, Prime Ministers, Churches and Royals are now the reiteration legacies of Africa and African-Caribbean people today. The impact on Africa and the Diaspora socially, economically, politically and psychologically cannot be overstated because Africa is still being raped daily and Africa has not progressed technologically and scientifically at all. The economical commixture is a serious situational problem. Whatever avenue we take, the delineation of the slaves struggles and liberation must be taken into account at all levels of thinking. The tabulation for this account is as follows:

1) Historical Evidence

There is no historical evidence that the slaves ever accepted enslavement. The contrary is evident that the slaves from the inception of capture or kidnapping applied serious resistance and rebellions. The Pagan Europeans and British fabricated a theological and cultural lie that God created Africans to be slaves. The Liverpool declaration was that they had full justification to enslave Africans for their happiness. According to Wilkins the inhabitants of Africa were particularly primitive and uncivilized. The Europeans believed that they had the God given rights and entitlement to continue enslaving the Africans. Henry Wilkins was a pagan. If he had seen Egypt and her magnificent Pyramids built by Africans psychologically and intellectually he would be forced to think and act differently towards Black achievements and contributions. Mr. Robin Walker in his book "When WE Ruled" has given us tremendous evidence and readings on the history of Africans.

2) African Resistance and European Dis-empowerment

Dr. Stephen Small and Prof. James Walvin writing on African Resistance to 'Enslavement' said 'Though the slave trade was horrible- flagitious and morally repugnant it did not break the spirit, initiative or resilience of the Africans that suffered the rape of their societies and human resources.' Africans resisted their bondage from the moment of enslavement. They did, because ontologically freedom is God's gift to each individual and community of people.

Africans were psychologically and physically obdurate towards enslavement because the price of freedom was ontological and cosmologically validated by their God. There was no ambiguity or doubt to them that from the inception of capture, when they were kidnapped, chained and placed in yokes to the Castles and dungeons, the slaves relied upon their unconquerable spirit. Their indestructible spirit which was the embre says Dr. Richard Hart, which motivated the slaves Revolts and Rebellions so frequently in the West Indies and the Americas. Haiti is a very explicit demonstration of the inner spirit and call for freedom by the African slaves.

It is historically factual to point out that the whole transatlantic slave trade was dominated by rebellions and insurrections. Slaves recalcitrance towards their enslavement and forced labour. The extraction from economical and racial oppressions. There were many plots by the slaves to secure their freedom from slavery. The methods used by the slaves range from civil disobedience, strikes, illness-pretence, diseases, particularly run-away slaves such as the various maroons across the West Indies especially in Jamaica and various states in the USA .and Canada.

In considering the impact of dis-empowerment some historians in dealing with the Abolition movement placed great importance on William Wilberforce, the Quakers and infrequently mention Thomas Clarkson and Granville Sharpe, British Parliament and British Antislavery Movement. On the other-hand very little importance to the Slaves Rebellions and the un-economic function of slavery caused by the slaves-themselves according to Dr. Eric Williams theory of Soil erosion and over-production has been given due appreciative attention. But the major part which must at all times be in the focus is the Slaves Revolts and Rebellions .In order to delineate respect a list of these will be helpful. (Quobna Ottoban Eugoano) he was the first African slave to demand total abolition of the slave trade and emancipation of the slaves. The Authentic Narratives of Ukawsaw Gronnionsaw (1770) Ottobah Cugoano (1787) Olaudah Equiano (1781) Ignatius Sasncho (1781)

Phillis Wheatley (1753-1754) probably born on the Gambia River. These Africans writings including Phillis Wheately's Poem on (Poems on various Subjects) were Slave Narratives dynamite. They challenged to the economic and racial foundation the transatlantic slave trade in Africans and the institution of slavery. They called not like the British for gradual abolition but rather immediate abolition.

3) Slaves Revolts and Rebellions

To calculate the number of revolts is not easy and it depends largely on definition. In the USA there were approximately 250 revolts. However, revolts were much more frequent in the British colonies especially in Jamaica. The first Maroon War of 1730-40. In Antigua 1735-36. Stono's Rebellion in1739. The prodigious Tacky's Revolt in Jamaica in 1760 which obliterated about 60 white lives but the slaves price was over 400 slaves were killed. Some 500 were transported from Jamaica. Then there is the Maroon War of 1795-96 and we have also Fedor's Rebellion in Grenada in 1795. It is of paradoxical significance that the claimed Abolition date of 1807 is (false). The slave trade actually witnessed more rebellions than ever before which dictated the chronology for radical abolition rather than gradual abolition which was being advocated in London. We have the Bussa's Rebellion in Barbados in 1816 and followed by the Demerara (Guyana) revolt in 1823 and dramatically the emancipation slave revolt namely the Baptist War in Jamaica in1831-32. The co-ordinated symbiotic number was 20,000. The fourteen white deaths provoked a tremendous wave of brutal reprisal which was so characteristic of the whites that it cost over 500 slaves lives. This is a clear demonstration of white racism and bitter flagitiousness. It is the view of Dr. Richard Hart that the single death of Rev. James Smith by natural causes helped to further dictate the time-table for abolition. The most remarkable Revolution in the history of slaves rebellions in the Caribbean, which white historians tried to play down but thanks to C .L .R. .James in his book "The Black Jacobins was the Toussaint L'Ouverture and the San Domingo Revolution. In 1791. The San Domingo Revolution was the fundamental turning point for the slaves, Slavery and emancipation.. This Revolution led to the establishment of the independent black republic of Haiti.

Throughout the slave trade history most of the revolts were by slaves and leaders who did not accept slavery as dictated and inculcated by the enslavers and church leaders. However, it was not until 1838 that indigenous slaves took up arms for their liberation in Jamaica. There is not much difference between the slaves who had experienced the horrific transatlantic crossing and the indigenous slaves. Dr. Small and Prof. Walvin sought to create a distinction between the two groups. Both scholars were not deeply aware of the psychic-connections between slaves. There is however a marked difference in the USA. In the United States most of the slaves leaders including (Nat Turner) were young, literate, married and charismatic, men says Blassingamer.

4) African Religion and Slaves Resistance to Slavery

It took the Africans very little time to understand that what the European and British church leaders, philosophers and theologians called Christianity was the fundamental reason for their oppression, enslavement, exploitation and dehumanization. Their Christianity was a misguided religion. It was a religion that taught the Africans disunity, disrespect, distrust, and hate, brutality towards each other.

It was a religion without moral content and moral authority. It was a flagitious cultural-semantical religion. Having this understanding of Christianity, the slaves held on to their African beliefs, including Myalism.

At the same-time the slaves who were freed and those in bondage created their own churches as means of solidarity and defence.

Dr. Small and Prof. James Walvin asserted that "the consolidation and transformation of African Religion (Myalism) shaped and even challenged Christianity as a source of inspiration." Africans embraced African religion because of their spirited links with their ancestors, God and the world. It is significant to point out that the European and British claimed that African religious beliefs and traditions were primitive. It was facinorous and fundamentally wrong and a deliberate fabrication by the Europeans and the British. The historical fact is that the Africans were the first to have developed a Monotheistic Faith. The belief in One Supreme Being. This academic postulation is made by Prof. Gayraud S. Wilmore in his "Black Religion and Black Radicalism, An Interpretation of the Religious History of Afro-American People".

It is remarkable in the indagation of the transatlantic (Black African) slave trade, that the witnesses of the (Slaves Narratives) all conveyed the same message and experience. Their narratives related to the heinous egregious slave trade conjoined by white Christianity. The slaves began to challenge the morality of white Christianity. Concepts that were banned for the missionaries use such as peace, obedience, loyalty, manumission, forgiveness, liberty, justice, brotherhood and equality. But the missionaries were allowed to preach heaven and hell condemnation and damnation to the slaves. Paradoxically, the slaves were inculcated with the myth and culture that slavery was their just punishment and that it was only by obedience to their enslavers that they would succeed to heaven. These were contradictions and ambiguities to the slaves. Olaudah Equiano, Harriet Jacobs, Frederick Douglas, Phillis Wheately and Ignatius Sancho are only a exiguous number of the volume of slave narratives articulating the same message and experience that Christianity and Slavery were not morally and theologically incongruous. The slaves narratives challenged the fundamental tenants of Religion, God and Christianity.

The enslavers sought to eradicate completely African religious traditions and customs by imposing on the slaves white Christianity which was a flagitious semantical culture and by looking upon African religious tradition as demonic, superstitious and henotheistic. The slaves however, cultivated and maintained their African Religious traditions despite their brutal punishment. It is necessary to remind ourselves that the Moravian Church fought with Myalism in Jamaica for over 100years and in Virginia USA also for over 100 years. The perennial struggles was for religious dominance. The slaves created churches fundamentally for spiritual, entrenous and psychological reasons. The spiritual and cultural connections were important for their survival. In addition to the claim above relating to Myalism, we can safely dogmatize and empiricize that Black Religion is part of the African slaves religion. The slaves even used the churches as a means of escape in the expression of their manumission. They used the churches to organize themselves for physical escape. The slaves knew that the enslavers Christianity and religious practices were egregious and pure profligateness. Equally for the slaves, the churches were the major engine of the slave trade through the rapid proliferation of white Christianity.

Women played a significant function in the manumission struggles in that the women had their own movement which was to guarantee them the unity and determination not to perpetuate slavery. They formed particular groups and forces. Benevolent associations in order to provide for themselves self-help. To the extent that they took care of each other and where there was death or sufferings and poverty they came together to alleviate the pressures of those unfortunate sisters. Their second and remarkable task was to consolidate themselves to abolish slavery. For the sake of information only, "women in Britain formed antislavery groups and movements, while William Wilberforce voted and campaigned against women freedom or political involvement in the abolition movement in Britain."

Dr. Small and Prof. Walvin shared the argument with Dr. Akbar in his book "Breaking the Chains of Psychological Slavery' that the churches sowed the seeds of discord among the slaves especially those with black congregations.' Collectively, Religion provided the frame-work for black religion to form developments for black congregations as a source of organization and self-expression. The church was the main place for the slaves to "grok" talk about their problems but essentially about slavery and abolition.

The white church leaders repeatedly sowed the seeds of discord as a means of control. The churches taught black slaves how to hate each other and again the churches and the slave trade institution were contiguous in their purpose of making the slaves eternally power-less through disunity. The white churches and the political powers and economic energy were not merely symbolical but they were effectively consolidated in the brutal transatlantic slave trade in African slaves. There are instances existentially and empirically that I am aware of that the established churches today continue with the same mentality and culture. In London there are churches that organize African groups against each other in the church, for mental and financial control of the African members. They make them compete against each other ruthlessly. Thereby reinforcing the philosophy of divide and rule which is basically part of the slave trade philosophy. Despite the relationship between the Church and the Political powers, the institution of slavery; through the Abolitionist movement, there were wide-spread under-ground movements, conspiracy was real but the power and energy came from the black slaves. Enslavement, brutal bondage, reduction to dis-empowerment in land and freedom, yet the slaves cultivated a tremendous sense and purpose of consanguineous bond religiously, socially, culturally and psychic- connection. The book "A History of Negro Revolt" by C. L. R. James is full of information on this aspect of the histographic accounts of the slave trade period.

Chapter 17

Disempowerment and Slaves Engagement

It should be apparent by now from the information articulated above that there is a massive myth that the slaves were made completely powerless by slavery and European and British Christianity. No doubt it was the fundamental reason for the ideology enmeshed in Racism and economic greed for the economies of Europe and Britain. But the opposite is apparent. The action of enforced enslavement by reason of destroying the slaves freedom, with the missionary instructions never to use the "words freedom, liberty, equality or manumission" to the slaves, but rather to instruct the slaves to accept their station of slavery without seeking manumission, in order to secure milk and honey in the hereafter. The missionaries argued that God had intended Africans to be slaves. It was another form of Racism. Their racial grounds for enslavement was with theological and psychological justification. This justification was purely psychological-disconnection or psychic-disconnection. But the systematic purpose and philosophy was disempowerment. There was a great ocean of incompleteness. The incompletion was the slaves spirit and will for persistent engagement which resulted ultimately in the slaves liberation from the institution of the brutal and barbaric slavery by Europeans and British alike. The slaves were engaged primarily in rebellions and insurrections. The engagement and writings of Equiano and Sancho and their abolition struggles are remarkable stories based on existential and empirical encounters in slavery itself. The narratives from the pens of the various slaves were powerful challenges to 'slavery' the institution and the Christianity of the missionaries, merchants, enslavers and traders. The slaves never formally accepted white Christianity. White Christianity had no moral meaning for the slaves. White Christianity had no function relating to liberation for the slaves. Rather, white Christianity was oppression and enslavement acted out in routinization enforced on the slaves flagitiously.

It was the psychological, spiritual and physical engagement which made the participation in the slaves liberation effective. Engagement took the form of individual engagement, symbiotic engagement and the amelioration of their shared experience of slavery bond the slaves stronger as slaves. The slaves were faced and confronted by the planters/enslavers and the acting out of racism. Racism expressed in theological, sociological, anthropological and psychological terms by the missionaries, church leaders, theologians and philosophers. Disconnection or psychic-disconnection was the form and function of endemic racism. There was at the same-time the pandemic spread of Maroon Wars throughout Jamaica, and South America. These are solid demonstrations of the slaves determination and objectives in their engagement to abolish slavery. The evilness and moral repugnancy of Slavery enmeshed in European and British Christianity and the affirmation that slavery was consistent with Christianity. The planters and enslavers saw no incongruity between slavery and Christianity because it was a semantical-cultural Christianity based on a slave system of flagitiousness. The evilness was the system and institution of slavery perpetuated by the Missionaries.

Missionaries which were the power-house and engine of the Transatlantic slave trade had psychic-dis- connections. It was the persistent engagement of the slaves which made manumission possible. The James Somerset case with Lord's Mansfield had marked Judgement showed that James Somerset was engaged. He was dis-empowered through slavery but he used the method and personal engagement to secure legally his freedom from enslavement. James Somerset was helped by Granville Sharp, Equiano and Sancho.

Alissandra Cummins looked at the situation of slavery carefully and he made this poignant observation. "The plantation system defined an ideology of racism which developed and grew throughout the period of slavery. Its devastating effect is still entrenched in Caribbean society today- three hundred years of human existence translated into economic and political power for the planters, social and economic degradation for the slaves. Rigid stratification ensured the degeneration of the African condition." It was the slaves themselves who changed their existential-empirical conditions of slavery through resistance and engagement. The myth of white superiority and black dependence was nurtured by forced compliance to dominant groups." One such group was the churches of which the Methodist explicitly claimed with theological justification for the divine biological ordination with justification of African enslavement.

Chapter 18
Slaves Audacity and Disempowerment

Dr. Richard Hart in his scholarly volumes 1&2 Slaves Who Abolished Slavery: Volume 1. Blacks in Bondage and Slaves Who Abolished Slavery Volume 2 Blacks in Rebellion. Dr. Hart has helped us with his brilliant accounts of the number of rebellions and the struggles of the slaves, especially the 20,000 who died. Dr. Hart has systematically articulated with his scholarship the great contributions of the slaves in their audacity towards enslavement and disempowerment. It was by their physical and psychological engagement that they confidently resisted their bondage and enslavement. What is of the greatest importance is that Dr. Hart has demonstrated that the slaves rebellions and other forms of resistances contributed significantly to their liberation, abolition of the slave trade and emancipation from slavery.

The traditional arguments of the culture of moral high ground by the British, the Evangelical Movement and the Enlightenment contributed to the Abolition of Slavery are untenable. Recent eximious scholarships and critical indagation into the transatlantic slave trade in Africans revealed the mendacious culture behind these historical postulations. Recent scholarships including the author of this thesis have shown that it was not the actual case. Abolition of the slave trade in Africans was not immediate termination of slavery. There were two schools on the abolition movement. One school advocated "gradual abolition." This was the view held that the slaves needed proper preparation for their freedom. The second school advocated immediate abolition. The Abolition Act of 1807 slavery by Britain and America in 1808 became more expansive and aggressive. Slavery was replaced with Apprenticeship and Peonage. However, Apprenticeships and Peonage were still slavery because the slaves had no freedom nor the restoration of their dignity. It was slavery by another name.

Some scholars lately are taking a more honest look at the slave trade in the light of new scholarships and radical approach to the subject. The author in this thesis is writing not so much literal history of the transatlantic slave trade but rather the approach is basically hermeneutical. Without a radical hermeneutical approach the inner rock of the subject will not be understood or exposed fully. It is only with the extrication from cultural and academic bias that the rectitude in scholarship will shine through. It must be reiterated that it was the slaves themselves through their revolts, insurrections and revolutions that created the road for their own freedom. And the beginning of the long process to restoration and manumission.

The extraordinary revolutionary personalities male and female recognition is in the dynamic effects of the Slaves Narratives. These need immortalization in symbols, writings, Libraries and museums. It is seriously important especially in the philosophy of Pan-Africanism and Reparation. Those who have sacrificed their lives in order to eradicate the burden of slavery must be memorialised in different forms. It is eternally important for modern day African-descendants to be informed of these audacious men and women. As Dr, Nkrumah reminded the people of Ghana in December 1958 that the Diaspora are part of us. He said "These sons and daughters of Africa were taken away from their shores and they have not forgotten their ancestral links… Long before many of us were conscious of our own degradation these men fought for African national and racial equality… Now that we in Africa are marching towards the complete emancipation of this continent, our independent status will help in no small measure their efforts to attain full human rights and dignity as citizens of their Country." Pan-Africanism and Regionalism by Prof. S.K.B. Asante. The J. B. Danquah Memorial Lecture March 2007 is a brilliant articulation of the history.

Immortalization and Memoralization of the revolutionary leaders have not received the attentions due to them historically. Below I will attempt to give some canon and justice to a few of these brave men and women. These remarkable slave leaders were deeply inspired by myalism and their inner desideration for freedom. To recover their ontological liberty and equality. Freedom which had been denied them through enslavement and disempowerment. The slaves were culturally, socially, religiously, economically, psychologically and sociologically raped by Europeans and British through slavery. Their humanity was violated and raped. They were forcefully subjugated. It was the imposition of slavery which oppressed and raped Africans of their humanity and dignity. African slaves were sodomized daily: men, women and children. They were sodomized in the name of Almighty God, a white Jesus Christ and a white semantical-cultural European and British Christianity.

Nigel Sadler has helped us with his study of slaves contributions in his book "The Slave Trade." Sadler acknowledged that slaves Rebellions as Dr. Hart claimed had played a remarkable and dynamic function in the opposition to slavery which was in essence and reality disempowerment of a race called Africans. (Black Race) External forces for the slaves was enslavement based on racism and economic superiority. Resistance by the slave leaders was against their legal status of slaves and properties. The legal status of slaves robbed them of their freedom. Slavery in Africans was done by the will of the British Parliament and Politicians. It was done with the support of the Royals, Planters, Merchants, Theologians, Philosophers, Archbishops, Bishops, Missionaries and Anthropologists.

The Churches had based their Theology of Racism which was a culture of superiority firmly on a Theology of Infralapsarianism. It was a doctrine based on a Theology of the elect and the damned by God.

That whites were the elect of God and that Africans were the damned by God. This Theology dominated the Liverpool Slave Trade philosophy and theology. Liverpool Capital of the Slave Trade by Gail Cameron and Stan Crooke. Covering the Company of Merchants trading to Africa established by an act of Parliament passed in the 23rd year of George 11. entitled "Act for Extending and Improving the Trade to Africa" belonging to Liverpool. June 24th 1752. The missionaries inculcated this doctrine on the slaves that slavery was ordained by God for them. Even the Methodist Minister of Religion and Professor of History at Kent University Prof. Roger Anstey had formulated the theory that "The enslavement of Africans was part of God's Salvation History." Prof. Anstey had not fully elucidated what he meant by "God's Salvation History."

With slavery and the culmination of disempowerment the slaves did not anticipated any imprecations for alleviation of their sufferings. With sagacious leadership and co-operative efforts they planned their revolts, uprisings and rebellions. These insurrections were frequently suppressed ruthlessly by the enslavers and merchants. Transatlantic slavery was based on brutality and psychic-distance. Slavery was the embodiment of British and European racism transmitted in the system and institution of enslavement with religious approval. It was conducted in the name of Almighty God, Christianity and Jesus Christ.

Passive Resistance by the Slaves

For slaves to runaway, it was an act of resistance and revolt and it was a frequent pattern. It was also encouraged by the British in relation to the American War of Independence. Slaves were encouraged to runaway and join the British. The British promised the runaway slaves their freedom and settlement in Britain.

It is generally held by scholars and students of history that Mahatma Ghandi was the first to have started Civil Disobedience or Passive Resistance. The application of the philosophy of Passive Resistance began with the slaves. The philosophy of Non-Violence Movement activated by Dr. M.L .King during the USA Civil Rights Movement. Slaves used the philosophy in the forms of faking illness, Improper tools, some murdered their child or children. These were various and drastic measures to curtail slavery. Studies by the author of this thesis has shown that the killing of children by parents during the slave trade with the intention for them not to have to endure slavery, created for the slave-mothers infaticidezation traumatic syndrome. This was a common psychological and emotional trauma the female parents experienced. Some slaves poisoned their masters. Some slaves took poison in order to induced abortions. Some song according to their cultures and tradition songs that were meaningful for them in their context of slavery. The basis of the slaves plantation culture was the plan to dislocate slavery. For some slaves it was not easy to carry the infant child. Murder of the infant was preferred to the sufferings, the harrows and traumas of slavery. Whichever ways their actions took, it was for the extirpation of slavery no matter by what means necessary. Slaves were forced into extreme measures to bring about the end to slavery.

Rebellions of Significance

In the Caribbean region there were a number of rebellions, revolts, uprisings and insurrections. None can compare in power and achievement to the first revolt in 1701 in Hisponiola in Haiti. The rebellion began with the recondite name in history of Boukman who was deeply religious and an inspired man. The dynamic and charismatic leader Toussaint L'Ouverture was the messianic leader of his people. The Haitian rebellion had tremendous impacts on the French, the Spanish and the British. C.L.R. James has given us a tabulated historical account of the Haitian Rebellion. C.L.R.James book "The Black Jacobins" is an historical account of the Haitian Revolution which exposed the mendacities created by many historians. The three countries suffered greatly by the power of L'Ouverture revolution. Fear was pandemic throughout the region. America saw the serious potential to safety and control in the Caribbean region. It was a tremendous signal for the potential for inspiration and the creation or motivation for audacity and philistinism to spread rapidly throughout the Caribbean. Trepidation was in spation throughout the slave trade business. But this fear was more evident in the British colonies in the Caribbean. Other Islands could well join in the revolution movement.

There were complexities caused by the Haitian revolution. The real problem was how to confront perfidiousness deeds by the French with Napoleon. It was a political paradox and a political problematic combined. L'Overture was tricked by the French and he was captured and arrested and later died in France in 1803. Without any hesitation the mighty Jean-Jacques Dessalines continued the war with France, he was assiduous with his forces and in 1803 Dessalines forces pulverised France and with his remarkable success he became the leader of the new Republic.

Slaves were determined to free themselves from the bondage of slavery and those who runaway formed themselves into groups called Maroons. The Maroons created their own independent communities in places such as Guyana, Surinam Surinam, Florida and especially in Jamaica in the hills of the Blue Mountain.

When the British expelled the Spanish from Jamaica the slaves who were Maroons fought the British successfully. They had more advantage than the British because their main base was in the hills. The war between the Maroons and the British lasted over forty years. The main area for the Maroons was St. Andrew in the hills of the Blue Mountains.1655, But the first major slave war which was the Maroon war was led by the immortal Cudjoe and Nanny of the Maroon. They were leaders and had developed communities in 1690. At the Black Rio Grande Valle. The British failed to obliterate the Maroons and they were forced to signed a treaty in 1739 and the British recognized the Maroons as a free people and even Nanny was given 500 acres of land from the Jamaican Government.

Chapter 19
The Second Maroon War 1795

The Second Maroon was between the British and the Maroons and the British attitude to the treaty proved to be a very perfidious treaty. The British reneged on the treaty and had the Maroons deported rapidly to Sierra Leone. The breaking of covenants is a characteristic feature of the British culture and religion.

The Third War was far more decisive in contents, mission and purposes. The Baptist War of 1831-2 led by the immortal Sam Sharpe, who was a Baptist preacher. For some scholars Sharpe was inspired by the Baptist movement but I beg to differ radically. Sam Sharp like other charismatic leaders of the day, were deeply moved henotheistically by Myalism which was an African religion of great historical importance. It was because of this historical importance to the Africans that the Moravian Church sought to obliterate Myalism in Jamaica. 600,000 Jamaicans were consolidated in this dramatic war. 30,000 enslaved workers took part in the ten day war revolt. 340 people were executed for taking part. But only 14 whites were killed. Here is the evidence that with any revolt which failed, the consequence was clearly racially defined by the measure of brutality, oppression and domination. There is also Nanny Griggs 1816 who set up militant actions against Slavery because she believed that all humans are born free. Finally, there is the Carlota Rebellion. She led the Triumvirato sugar plantation workers in a revolt and she and others were killed. Zumbi he too had a revolt but he was killed. At his capture he was beheaded.

In 1763 Cuffy (Kofi) he led a slave revolt in Guyana, this revolt lasted for ten months but because of mordacious dis-agreements between the group and the precipitation of Kofi's, end came with him causing suicide followed by the dissipation of the rebellion.

In the USA approximately 2000 slave revolts and conspiracies between 1600-1865 took place. In 1800 Cabriel Arosser had planned to march on Richmond Virginia. But betrayal was also a major marker. As in the case of Vessey in 1822. He was betrayed and he and other leaders were brutally hanged. This plot was prodigiously planned. But the most successful revolt in the USA was that of the immortal Nat Turner in 1831. He succeeded in killing his master's family. Turner was eventually captured and hanged.

Chapter 20
Escape- Movement

The slaves used the methods of Revolts and Rebellions very effectively in many ways, but the mordacious way to hurt the enslavers was to escape. We have seen that the Maroons had perfected the method of escape. To escape was economically effective. Escapee such as Harriet Jacob who ran away created pell-mell to her enslavers. She used her limited freedom to educate herself and to write her own slave narrative "Incidents in the Life of a Slave Girl Written by Herself." Because escapes by slaves was difficult they needed real assistance and this led to what became known as the (Underground Railroad Movement) The best story is that of Harriet Tubman. For many years after Tubman escaped slavery in 1849 Harriet made nearly 100 trips to the South endangering her life and helping over 300 slaves escaped to freedom in the North. She helped her brothers, sisters and parents. She was a great hero to the enslaved. She was never caught and she became known as the Moses of her people.

Harriet Jacobs Incidents in the Life of a Slave Girl Written by Herself in 1861 is a remarkable lived story of a slave girl. The Introduction written brilliantly by Professor Nell Irvin Painter Professor of American History at Princeton University USA. Harriet Jacobs demonstrated the two areas of this thesis in her feminist embodiment. Disempowerment and Engagement. The brutal grip of slavery made the conscious slaves actively engaged in the process of their liberation. Jacobs especially emphasized the destructive assault on slaves psyches. In my book "The Psychological Combination of Christianity and Slavery. The impact on African-descendant's psyche" I identified the traumatic syndromes created on the slaves by the ruthlessness of slavery. Harriet Jacob has narrated some experiences that are pertinent and germane to this thesis.

Harriet described the powerful grasp of her condition as the "demon of Slavery" She was completely powerless by the slave system which defined her by law as chattel. She was equally powerless in dealing with her senior white citizen James Norcom. To circumvent her dilemma she "made a headlong plunge" into a sexual relationship with Sawyer. Jacobs insists that enslaved black women cannot be judged by the same standards as the free. She elucidated the conditions of enslavement that deprived people of autonomy, denying them influence over their own and their children's destiny.

Jacobs addresses her readers pellucidly in Incidents: "You never knew what it is to be a slave; to be entirely unprotected by law or custom; to have the laws reduce you to the condition of a chattel, entirely subject to the will of another" It is. important to note that in 1831 Nat Turner led his insurrection in Southampton Virginia. Dr. Painter says "On the pretext of searching for insurrectionists, white men looted, beat, raped, murdered, and generally terrorised African- Americans."

Dr. Painter commenting on Incidents in the Life of a Slave Girl says "it is first and foremost a piece of engaged writing, a means of advancing the struggle against the institution of slavery by politicizing respectable Northern white women as women. Painter made it clear that Harriet wrote straight facts, with no fiction. Because it was her existential and empirical journey. Harriet was disempowered by the institution of slavery, but she engaged herself in the struggles for the abolition of slavery.

Harriet Jacobs disempowerment and engagement like Frederick Douglas tells the impacting story that slavery was demonic, ruthlessly evil and a deeply facinorous system perpetuated by the churches. From her story, the story of Frederick Douglas, the story of Olaudah Equiano, the story of Ignatius Sancho and many others. Africans and Africans Diasporas must conclude that disempowerment has made Africans powerless. That it destroyed the collectiveness of African-descendants. It has made Africans and Diasporas into individuals which in itself is powerlessness, rather than collective-connected Africans and Diasporas which would make African-descendants great, with strength, respect, power and dignity. I believe that the slaves narratives were not chimerical narratives but lived narratives. There is nothing canty with sodality about slave narratives. Rather their narratives are graphic, mordacious and gripping stories of men and women created in the nature, character and personality of God. The God who is the Ground-of-our-Being.

The sum total of these remarkable stories and great events of the history of black slavery is that both men and women were courageous people struggling for their freedom in the midst of a horrendous, immoral, flagitious system and institution. It tells of the African race outstanding nature and spirit. But most importantly, it tells the story that black people from the beginning knew God. It is this spiritual relationship with God which cannot be defined in anthropological and anthromorphic languages that defined Black Spirituality as unique. The autobiography of Harriet Jacobs is one effeminate illustrious story of a black slave girl's survival, engagement and strength. An additional admission is that "Black" people are living with the reiteration legacy of disempowerment, paralysis, and enslavement psychologically, sociologically, economically, theologically and politically improvident and impuissant. These terminologies are calmatives in effects, impacts and meaning.

It is factual historically that the slaves experienced disempowerment at its crudest but the slaves applied their natural engagement desideration of inner conflagration of manumission from the bondage of slavery, oppression, dehumanization and powerlessness. It was this tremendous sense and purpose of engagement that created all the philosophical and psychological differences to the slaves. White historians have tried to hide the truth (recondite) that it was the slaves that made their own pathway to freedom possible. It had nothing to do with morality on the part of the enslavers. Compassion was radically absent from their vocabulary. It must be a timely reminder that the enslavers had no psychic-connection with African humanity. It follows therefore that the enslavers also had no spiritual-connection with a morally good, merciful and compassionate God. They were basically pagans walking with incorrigibility and flagitiousness.

Chapter 21
Pan-Africanism Vs Disempowerment

Under-development is a system of the legacies of disempowerment and the European and British stratification in the institution of slavery to both create and to make African-descendants permanently dis-empowered and powerless with paralysis. But Quobna Ottoban Coggon who was captured into slavery as a child and transported to the West Indian island of Grenada he was the first African to demand the total abolition of the slave trade and emancipation of slaves. He experienced the heinous power of slavery as dis-empowerment but he engaged himself for his liberation and empowerment.

For any significant change to be effective it must begin and come from the consciousness of the nation, individual or community. Before Kwame Nkrumah made his voice known, people such as Du Bois, Marcus Garvey and George Padmore were the original pioneers of Pan Africanism who saw and understood the philosophy of Pan-Africanism V Disempowerment. MR. Henry Sylvester Williams historical place in history is well secured. The fundamental focus and light was within the dictum "We predict that Africa will always remain what it has always been-the black man's continent. There may be fringes of population of whites here and there, but the main bulk of the people will be black. We talk of Boer and Britain in South Africa, as if that were a statement of the whole matter. What if, at some distant date in the future, South Africa should belong neither to Boer nor Britain, but to the Negro-his by right, by superior numbers, and superior power? We may smile at the right superior numbers, and superior power? We may smile at their idea, but it may become a tremendous reality."

In March 2007 Dr. S.K.B. Asante delivered the J.B. Danquah's Memorial Lecture series 40 on the title "Ghana and the Promotion of Pan-Africanism and Regionalism." It was a lecture punctuated and articulated with eximious scholarship. Dr. Asante elucidated with acknowledgement the historical genesis of the concept and philosophy of Pan-Africanism. The significance of Padmore from Trinidad and Marcus Garvey from Jamaica are looked at in terms of their great contributions to the Movement of Pan-Africanism. The figure of par-excellence is Kwame Nkrumah the first President of Ghana. Nkrumah fundamental appeal was "Africa must Unite" Nkrumah appeal was not welcomed by the West namely Britain and America. It is important to keep the knowledge and consciousness alive by reminding ourselves that Britain functioned on the political premise of divide and rule. Therefore Nkrumah appeal and philosophy would have had a lukewarm welcome. A political Laodicea- welcome. Pan-Africanism is to be understood from the direct specific purposes relating to Africa.

The Diaspora

The personalities of Patmore, Garvey and Nkrumah appealed to the Diaspora was lambently made, but when examined critically it is easy to see its fallacious and psychological connection along with the psychic-connection only as a epistemological dream The Diasporas must be educated people for this task. They must be symbiotic in desire, determination and philosophy. The connection can be through proper information, through consciousness-connection. Some Diasporas had a basic mythological vision of Africa or Ghana. The mythological concepts are based on the education they have had. Their cultural orientation is also a major problem for them to overcome.

The most astonishing argument of Dr. Asante for the Diaspora is that Diasporas people should be allowed to return to Ghana (home) with their finance. His thesis is tantamount to all that he is looking for and expecting from the Diasporas is (Finance). His thesis and philosophy of Diasporas people is fundamentally illogical, lacking in rectitude, lacking in respect, and most importantly it is a delineation of the absence of what is so important namely the psychic-psychological connection which was destroyed by the heinous transatlantic (Black African) slave trade for 500 years. It is necessary to correct Dr. Asante thesis immediately before his polluted and jejune thesis begin to germinate or begin to spread. First Dr. Asante is fundamentally wrong and his thesis is endemically facinorous. He clearly does not understand Pan-Africanism and the Diasporas. The only language Africans understand is (Money) (Finance) Aids. These I have looked at under Reparation. His thesis is based on rapscallionism.

For Ghana or indeed Africa to make any significant progress that will demand respect nationally and internationally from the West or so-called developed countries Ghana and the rest of Africa needs the following radical remedies and particularly accountable domestic leaderships.

Radicalization Approach

Africa must continue to be a black man's continent. As Danquha made very clear "We must as soon as practicable have autonomy or self-government, Our colonial status must be abolished. With self-government we shall be able to speak of our government as "Our Government" and Executive or Cabinet of the Gold Coast that refused to do the will of the people, could be made to cease to be the Executive or Cabinet in a day's general election. The case for African freedom is a cast iron case."
Africa must Unite. This was the call of the immortal Nkrumah. It is absolutely imperative for Africa to unite as a continent. Dynamic transformation must be effectuated. To continue as they are because of poor and oppressive leadership, corruption and selfishness. (Europe was once dis-united) today there is the European Union now merging as a powerful economic world power. Africa must have political-unification for the 21st century.

Ghana needs Diaspora people not necessary for their "finance" which is a shameful suggestion according to Dr. Asante. Diaspora people needs to return to Africa with their (a) Their experiences and professionalism. It is with these values and imperatives that Ghana and Africa will change significantly in comprehensive developments for its people.

The sociological, economical and psychological impacts of the transatlantic slave trade and colonialism is endemic in Ghana and throughout Africa. This area needs careful study, research and implementation urgently. It must be a consolidated effort and purpose by the governments, people and especially African Diasporas from all walks of life professionally.

Psychologically the people of Africa still believe in the West. They continue to see Britain, Europe and America as their ultimate canon always. Self-confidence is still lacking. In looking to Britain, Europe and America the psychological and economical expectations are based on charity and aids. Charity ethically and morally in the reiteration of the transatlantic slave trade legacies is a philosophy filled with dangerous consequences for Africa. It strangulates development and continues the cementation of dependence.

Pan-Africanism is the transformation and radicalization of the consciousness of the people. Africa for most people in Europe, Britain and America means under-development and a perpetual begging basket. The perception is maintained by the various images on T.V. The images are not all false. Most are self-inflicted by oppressive governments and endemic corruption. Africa needs psychological, educational and sociological radical changes immediately.

In November 2009 China offered Africa 10, billion dollars loans. What the African leaders are not aware of is that China will extract 50-75 billions dollars in natural resources and dumping of inferior products from China in abundance that will inundate Africa. This type of trade deal is in keeping Africa in the grip and wheels of strangulation. Furthermore, according to the political mentality of African leaders. The 10, billion dollars will not create a significant dent in Africa in terms of infrastructure improvements and developments. Politically and economically they will have no reciprocal tangible in ostentation for the money.

Pan-Africanism as a basic philosophy of Unity and a call on the Diasporas for the collective development of Africa must be a significant call for all Africans. It must be a psychological call. A call to consciousness. A call with moral and social rectitude. Far too many Diasporas people and likewise the indigenous returned back overseas with bitter stories and experiences. Most of the indigenous people are of the mentality that Diasporas people are stupid. The transatlantic slave trade heterogeneous mentality is deeply endemic in the African culture. It is a culture based on selfishness and narrow-mind-ness.

The voice of a young man is still meaningful today. We have finished the war physically, but morally it is not over. We have to struggle for liberty; at home the suppression is great. We have been spared back to life from the fighting front: but unless God gives us grace we shall fight to death about the suppression mode of rule we are encountering out here. In comparison we are regarded less human: as our lowliness in this sphere of the world, it is worse… We have made up our minds to help build the country, free from oppression, and in our oath to the Lord, we shall never miss you in all our plans to build our motherland.

Chapter 22
Elucidation of Pan-Africanism

Pan-Africanism literally understood is the promulgation of George Padmore, Sylvester Williams, Marcus Garvey and Kwame Nkrumah ideological philosophy. In reality today, Pan-Africanism Diasporas ought to be based on the spontaneous peregrination of the Diasporas. The essential philosophy of Pan-Africanism is the encouragement to know that with the Past-Present- and Future with people of the same ethnological commixture are inter-connected. Furthermore Pan-Africanism is ideological and strangely it is deeply epistemological dreaming. Realization of Pan-Africanism lies within the concept of Pan-Africanism itself. Culturally, psychologically, politically and theologically.

People are by nature-heuristic economically and sociologically. It is biblical and relevant to the story of Abraham in the Old Testament in the Bible. Abraham's migration was economical to the story. Next Abraham was motivated by economical improvidence. The biblical redactors gave the Abraham's story a religious and theological elucidation.

Pam-Africanism can only come into freedom and fruition through the radical general development of Africa, that is through social developments, economical developments, stable-democratic political leadership, educational development, agricultural development, psychological liberation and development. Radical reduction in the cultural heterogeneity of ethnic groups. Transformation of the endemic culture of charity. The expectation to be receivers with a culture of rapscallion. Then there is the culture of the poor/poverty in the midst of abundant natural resources and congenial climatic conditions. Through scientific and technological advancement for the development of all Africans and African-descendants. The political and radical removal of endemic corruption, selfishly motivated by the force of individual rapacity. Lastly Pan-Africanism is possible only through and when Africa is 'United' with political unification.

Fundamental psychological and intellectual re-thinking of what it means to be sagacious. There is a pandemic social culture with most Africans that they think they are astute/ sagacious than African-descendants from the Diasporas. They do not understand what sagacity is all about with rectitude. What social-anthropologist called 'Rapscallion' This concept and philosophy of being smart is tantamount to be liars and crooks. This is nothing more than a culture of rapscallion. It is not related to be a brilliant Engineer, Mechanic, Scientist, Technician or Designers, Sociologist or Psychologist. The concept of being scamps/ lies behind Dr. Asante argument that the Diasporas should return only with their finance. His argument has nothing to do with developmental experiences and expertism/ professionals.

Political leaders need reminding that it is said that slavery was abolished over 200 years ago and Africa as a continent has not developed significantly and improved scientifically and technologically. These are the fundamental areas for concentration by African countries and Africa as a continent.

Draw-backs

Africa has never built an aeroplane, helicopter, war-ships. Africa has no space programme. No Nuclear Project. No heavy duty vehicles, proper cold storage, submarines and proper infrastructures. Most general Hospital in Ghana are sub-standard, because of politics. While the poor people are suffering. The infrastructures are dated and colonially dated.. Irrigation and proper sewage drainage are seriously needed. The lack of proper and modern facilities are central to the health problems and malaria. This inefficiencies in good health and environmental services and facilities are the reasons for un-told un-necessary deaths each year. The national Hospital in Accra is a good example. The irrigation system is ancient. Diasporas are willing to return back to Africa but not to live at sub-standard level. First economically Diasporas needs to be paid at the same or better salary grade than in Europe, Britain or America. Drastic and Radical changes are possible with the experiences of Diasporas.

Africa is comparatively backward, this is both sociological and technological. It is the reiteration of the transatlantic slave trade legacies. The question of imperativeness is, is Pan-Africanism and Regionalism practical? The social, educational and economical policies needs correcting immediately. Diasporas living in Europe, Britain, USA, Canada and Australia with the challenges of racism and institutionalized racism should return to Africa to live below their difficult social standards. The reiteration of the transatlantic slave trade policy and philosophy of permanent dis-empowerment and powerlessness is a major legacy. Africa has not yet began to confront; face up-to. Pan-Africanism must face the challenges existentially head on. It is collective and symbiotic challenges. The urgency is the creation of a nation's psychological consciousness. Rather, the continent of Africa needs to have a national consciousness based on Pan-Africanism and political consciousness.

A region of Australia in November 2009 was experiencing serious water supply due to: (a) Not enough water flowing into the lake. (b) Serious drought in the area reducing the supply in volumes. The Australian government and farmers spent millions of dollars in laying large pipes from a river to supply water to the lake. The people of the area began to live their lives as before. Restoration of their lives.

In Africa a major ecological climatic condition is drought. Many governments failed to build dams and lakes in anticipation of droughts. But they are always very busy buying inferior guns from Britain, Europe and the USA to fight and to kill each other. Several wives and B M. W. cars. At the same time the African leaders are making fundamentally Africa poorer. A report on the fighting in the Congo appeared on the TV in 2008. There were five men looking for gold in a gully river. There was one white man on a hill looking down at them mining for gold. He has a ten bed room house. The men were mining for gold to buy guns to fight the opposition side. Their wives and children were starving at the same-time. This mentality is a major problem in Africa and the lack of accountable transparent leadership in the name and language of transparency.

Chapter 23
Pan-Africanism and Typology

There are many legacies of the Transatlantic slave trade ranging from (The Reiteration existential legacies of the transatlantic middle passage slave trade. The various traumatic syndromes suffered by the slaves.) The representations are of the African Diaspora and it does include the dynamic diversity of cultures and cultural interactions permeating throughout the Americas, Europe and Britain. The most distinguished and recognisable cultural legacy is black music of African origin. The Rhythm is spontaneous and dynamic. There are several types of music which are traceable back to slavery. For example the Drums used in Samba music which was accepted by the Brazilian enslavers. While in the USA there were great trepidation of the use of the drums. The drums were looked upon as a means of communication by the slaves.

The paradigms of West African influence was the storytelling community and tradition, encapsulating characters and images such as Anansi the spider and Brabbit or wily rabbit. Prof. Ann C. Bailey in her impressive book African Voices of the Atlantic Slave Trade, she relied on oral tradition, transmission and Story- telling. Contemporary legacies are delineated by the major Carnivals, Masquerades and Junkanoo performances which are common place legacies throughout the Caribbean Islands. It is also active in Ghana West Africa, USA and Europe. These legacies ought not to be taken lambently but rather with the appreciation of their deep roots in Africa. Even in 1811 Dowson a Methodist missionary wrote of the great celebrations in the Islands.

Europeans and British alike sought diligently and assiduously to justify theologically with the aid of Christianity. The Anglican Church in the 18th century called for an international conference to discuss the theological justification of slavery. The Methodist Church on the other-hand claimed theological justification for slavery. The Methodist Church also claimed that doctrinally Africans were biologically ordained to be slaves. Economically and politically the general justification by Europeans and the British was that slavery was the medium through which Africans and African-descendants could come into Christianity. That enslavement and Christianity functioned concomitantly. Theologically it was a diabolical contradiction because the slave trade or transatlantic slave trade had a developed theology of Infralapsarianism. It was not a doctrine as such. It was oppression, exploitation, human sufferings and alienation. This theology was based on the elect (whites) and the damned by God (Africans).

European and British Christianity was a Christianity based on inculcation at the expense of the repudiation of all African traditional Religions and Religious beliefs, especially Myalism. Myalism had for some considerable time, had a tremendous season of vicissitudes and challenges with the Moravian Church for over 100 years in America and Jamaica. The great struggle was for domination and the eradication of the African Religious traditions.. It was also a culture fighting against an old African religious tradition. What has been seriously overlooked is that the Moravian Church represented European heathenism and paganism. Sadly, the Africans assimilated and acculturated European Christianity with African religious beliefs. It was on the other-hand one way of mitigating their brutal suffering and oppression. The great and unwitting danger was that Africans accepted European white Saints or Christian Saints, which were reinforced by Europeans religious denial of African religious paradigms such as St. Augustine. In addition all the African Religious Early Church Fathers and the Biblical characters.

The slave owners feared African religion because of the possibility for the slavers to organise and have meetings, including individual thought and ensembling. Disunity, disrespect and hate were inculcated in the slaves for each other, The philosophy of the enslavers were the making of the Africans consistently powerless and disempowered persistently. African Unity or the call for Pan Africanism was not encouraged. Methodism and Baptists appealed more to the slaves than Anglicanism and Catholicism. Where African culture was given a limited degree of manumission, the enslaved kept their African religion and we can see this in Brazil today where there are millions of followers among the Diasporas. There is also the influence in the Ashanti in Kenta cloth which is a representation of history, philosophy, ethics, oral literature, moral, religious and political ideology.

Ronald Segal in his seminal thesis ‘The Black Diaspora’ has reminded us of the depth of Racism within the religious culture of Britain, the philosophical culture of Britain and the political culture of Britain. Blacks were in Britain more than a thousand years before the commencement of the transatlantic slave trade. There were African soldiers in the Roman army. (Septimius Severns 210) Queen Elizabeth 1 was profoundly disturbed by the African presence in Britain that in 1601 the Queen issued a proclamation stipulating the forceful expulsion of blacks as infidels and as an economic burden on Britain. The illustrious champions of the Black slaves in Britain were such immortals as Olaudah Equiano who worked with Granville Sharp on the murder of 132 slaves thrown alive in the sea from the Liverpool ship Zong. Next to Olaudah Equiano or Gustavas Vassa was Ottobah Cugoano. He joined forces with Equiano and Sharp. Ottobah Cugoano published his book entitles (Thoughts and sentiments on the evil and wicked traffic of the slavery and commerce of the human species). 1787. his book had a tremendous impact on the Antislavery movement.

The philosopher John Locke, the intellectual founder of the political commitment to the inalienable rights of man in his Essay 'Concerning Human Understanding' delineated in his writings that the 'Negron' was not a man or human. At the same-time John Locke with deep distant-psychic, personally invested £600 in the slave trading Royal African Company. Equally the great eighteen-century philosopher of empiricism David Hume postulated the concept of a 'natural white superiority.' The whole period of the transatlantic slave trade was based on European and British endemic Racism expressed especially in the rapid spread of white Christianity and slavery. Racism was pandemic in the various forms of academic scholarship. We see Wheatley's repudiation of the Society for the Propagation of the Gospel in her poem. Dr. Helen Thomas said "Wheatley's criticism of Quaque's activities, were not confined to a critique of his religious orthodoxy. Rather, it challenged his inherently ambiguous position as a Church of England missionary at a British Fort in Africa and by implication condemned the S.P.G.'s continued links with the commercial activities of the slave trade and colonialism."

It would be a great deception and misunderstanding for someone to say that slavery was abolished or ended in 1807. Instead, slavery moved into top gear by the British and the Americans after 1807. Colonization was the continuation of dis-empowerment, powerlessness and slavery. The indentured labours in the colonies and in the USA peonage was slavery by another name. However, Africa to day is in the grip of the reiteration legacies of the transatlantic slave trade. Negel Sadler said "The largest legacies of the Slave Trade is the situation in Africa today. The transatlantic slave trade in Africans depleted the African Continent of many of the young people, adults and stalled its development. Paradoxically, at the same-time, the slave trade in Africa was just the beginning of the colonial development of the continent and with the end of the European powers fought over Africans natural resources.

Dis-empowerment and persistent powerlessness is a fundamental reiteration of the transatlantic slave trade. Legacies affecting Africa, Pan Africanism and the Diaspora's is significantly enmeshed in the Transatlantic Slave Trade. The Diasporas has made strides globally in different spheres of human development economically and politically. The US Senior Scientist is from Ghana. The question therefore is, is this contribution acknowledged universally? Ghana like other African countries seem to export their intellectual developments worldwide through the Diasporas. Countries of recent extraordinary development, Europe, Britain and the USA are benefiting. While Africa remain static and in a state of stagnation, underdevelopment, dysfunctionalism and paralysis.

Africa is deeply gripped in the reiteration legacies of the transatlantic slave trade legacies. The real slavery today is in the form of economical development, scientific advancement, technological development, agricultural development transformed into aggre-power, psychological and sociological under-development. These are areas of bondage and slavery. These are the continuation of slavery and the exploitation of Africa's natural resources, China, Europe Britain and America only invest their interests where there are resources for exploitation Human chattle slavery is outdated. The transatlantic slave trade in Africans has been taken over by the economic enslavement of African Natural Resources. The African leaders, Chiefs and Kings who were attached to the transatlantic slave trade era, they were scoping off Africa's Natural Resources especially from the human perspective.

They are philosophically making slaves out of their system. No African leader would be allowed into Europe, Britain or the United States to exploit their gas, oil, Forests and Wild Life.. Africa has never had any Reparation paid by Europe, Britain or America. Plus the under-development of the whole Continent. We must not forget the 300,000.000 Africans who were murdered by slavery. The Jews constantly remind the world of what they themselves verified as 6,000.000 But historically they were Eastern European Jews. There are some schools of thinking that promulgate the concept that 'holocaust' is not the proper terminology. While the African transatlantic slave trade was the African holocaust. Prof. Shlomo Sand in his International Bestseller ' The Invention of the Jewish People' has open up for us a new world of scholarship which all readers and students of biblical history must take very serious.

Chapter 24
Africa - A Disempowered Continent

Africa is materially, economically, technologically, sociologically and psychologically a very indigent continent of people. Poverty is rampant pandemic-ally in Africa. Under-development is conspicuous and pandemic in Africa. Africa is very ineffective on the global stage technologically and economically. Africa has no symbiotic democratic voice of global recognition. Why? Because with the Berlin Conference of 1884-5 Europeans and the British met and together they carved up the Continent of Africa into individual countries specifically for the purpose of complete control and the creation of powerless-ness of Africa. It was done without any regard for the indigenous of Africa. It is a clear delineation of the weakness of African leaders. The historical leaders seemed not to have had any teeth. African Royals had never received any meaningful respect from Europeans and the British public. The culture of British domination, superiority and Racism has crippled Africa sociologically and psychologically. It is within these areas that we need to look for Africa's sociological, psychological, technological and economical empowerment. Before that can be done meaningfully there are a number of drastic and radical measures that must meet with combined effectuation. There must be the Pan-African will of the late Jomo Kenyatta. (Harambee) "Let's Pull Together. The call of Dr. Kwame Nhkrumah (Africa Must Unite) must be re-visited with the verve and philosophy of Pan-Africanism and the recognition of the Diasporas. 'Political Unification' is a must for African survival. This call for cultural and psychological radicalization of African-leaders and people's mind-sets is as urgent as the soteriological and eschatological call of the Messiah. "The Kingdom of God is at hand." Mark cp.1 V 15.

The European Union; A Political Power-house

African leaders can now begin to emulate aggressively and collectively the economical, political, sociological and technological power of the European Union if they were to have effective Political Unification.. The European Union presently is engaged in helping to draw a new map based on globalization and to shape the global economical landscape of economical and technological power. The European Union is looked upon and accepted by the USA, India and China as a united Union of people. These developed countries seem to accept Africa as the only place or avenue for natural resources to supply their rapacious culture and economic system from slavery to the present day.' Africa is still the European, British, China, Russian and USA dumping ground'. Dr. Walter Rodney's philosophy is still echoing loudly. 'How Europe Under-developed Africa'. Africa at the same-time is thought of by European and British as a continent to show their cultural Charity as economical and their characteristic placation of conscience for the 500 years of rape of African people in the name of Almighty God and Christianity. The European Union sees Africa as a vitally important source based on cheapness for the economies of Europe and Britain.

Within Europe there is the reciprocal necessity of shared technology and science. Political, economical and technological co-operation for the European economic community. All cultural and political differences are laid aside for the benefits of the community. The economy of Europe is tremendous. The eyes of Europe are on India and China both with billions of people driving hard their economical prosperity.

The African American Andrew Young has a significant approach to Pan-Africanism. For Young African productions and markets are essential to Africa's economical development. The developed countries needs to open up their markets more to Africa. Africa according to the late Dr. Walter Rodney is still the dumping ground of Europe's, Britain, China and India's cheap goods. Here lies the continuation and perpetuation of economical dis-empowerment. There is another dichotomy and paradox of importance. Africa is not only economically dis-empowered but principally Africa is psychologically dis-empowered. This is the major problem. The sociological and psychological enslavement is deep in the African psyche. Psychological liberation is necessary. Then economical, political and sociological liberation will automatically follow.

African leaders are not a combined force in the eyes of globalization economically. African leaders are permitting the continuation rape of Africa. The reiteration legacies are pandemic geographically in Africa. Ghana is the third largest Gold producing country in the world. Ghana has not got its own indigenous refinery. The real benefits are with foreign governments and countries. Nigeria is one of the largest Oil producing country in the world and its people and infra-structure in many parts are pri-mardia. The Congo is another major country with political and economical problems. Precariously the continent of Africa is under-developed. There is but limited presidium of representations. Serving the nation and the people is not the moral, social, economic and political priority. There is the culture of dependency and improvidence deep in the African psyche.

China and Japan have car plants in Europe, USA and Britain. These are car manufacturing countries. These are developed countries. These are technological countries. Africa is inundated with cars from these countries. There is no European car manufacture plant in Africa. There is no British car plant in Africa. There is no USA car plant in Africa. There is no China or Japan car plant in Africa. China and Japan frequently dumped their second-hand cars on Africa. In return they have a free hand on Africa's natural resources and forestations and wild-life. Africans cannot enter these countries freely and attempt to do anything without very limited and appropriate measures. The psychological enslavement is not only African based, it affects the whole global Diasporas.

By the perspective of reiteration the sociological and psychological impact of the transatlantic (Black African) slave trade demographically on Africa has never been evaluated educationally with recommendations for the betterment of the peoples of Africa. African countries are deeply gripped in the psychological bondage still of the slave trade legacies. Most African countries believe that their salvation is with Europe, Britain and the USA. The psychological bondage has encapsulated the Diasporas. African-Americans and in the twenty fist century the immigrants of African descendants are inter-locked with the Diasporas.

There is an African Union but its leadership has never been tested on the world stage of power and influence. Its basic problem is that Africa has not been able to transform the vast under-development of the continent. Africa has not shown any power of political and economical audacity. Africa's great dis-empowerment and powerlessness rest with Africa's ineffectiveness and incapability to repudiate and transform the reiteration legacies of the transatlantic slave trade impact of 500 years. It is a tremendous sociological and psychological bondage of slavery. The requirement is collective will-power to jettison the white-elephant legacies. Africa must create its own African common market. Africa must unite to bring all these epistemological dreams to pass. The Diasporas with intellect, experience and professionalism with the consciousness that all African-descendants are African's children. Connected consciousness as Diasporas a powerful way to move forward with confidence. Israel with 7 million people more or less dominate the Arab world with science and technology. Its strength is with the Jewish Lobby in the USA. Where is Africa's consolidated might and power? We talk about reparation in a fragmented way around the Diasporas. Africa as a black continent should collectively call upon Europe, Britain and the USA for reparation. Africa must fulfil positively its place in the world in order to woo the Diasporas to feel deeply psychologically connected with Africa.

Pan-Africanism and consciousness of the Diasporas is the way forward. The genesis is with education. African-conscious information. The proffer of combined solidarity with the Diasporas conscious connection to Pan-Africanism philosophy and goals. We acknowledged the profligation of the transatlantic slave trade and the sociological and psychological impacts slavery had on Africa. The movement must now be through the collective efforts to jettison the reiteration-legacies of the transatlantic slave trade. It is absolutely imperative and urgent. Africa needs men and women of the mind, character and indomitable courage of Albert Luthuli the South African Nobel Peace Prize winner in 1961.

Chapter 25
Demographical-Disempowerment of African descendants

Several white scholars are guilty of deliberately and racially fabricating false numbers or figures of Africans who died as a consequence of the transatlantic slave trade for 500 years. Dr. James Walvin, Dr. Herbert S. Klein, Dr. Basil Davidson to mention only a few. They have doctored the approximate authentic figures of the African slaves who died at the hands of profligate Europeans and British so-called Christians and Missionaries. Black people should remember and constantly reiterate the historical fact that European and British semantical cultural Christianity was deeply culturally, sociologically and theologically deeply flagitious. They quoted figures ranging between 15,000.000 to 50.000.000 The correct figure is 300.000.000.

Dr. Vincent Harding in his magnum opus claimed that approximately 100. 000.000 Africans died in the heinous transatlantic slave trade crossings.' Middle Passage' 'Kebuka' Even these figures are academically estimated.

But when we examined the records and purchases files especially 1) Auctions files. 2) Slaves coasts records especially Cape Coast Castle Ghana. 3) Slaves Dungeons records. 4) Records of those who died and those who choose the sea to the bondage of enslavement. 5) Those who died because of diseases and infections. 6) Those who died because of (a) Infibulation and (b) Imbrications on the ships. 7) Those who died from traumatic syndromes. 8) Those who died from whippings. 9) Those who ran-away and were killed by blood-hound dogs. 10) Those who died from over-work. 11) Those who died in the barracoons. 12) Those who died in the early period from the lack of ventilation. 13) Those who died from heartless sodomization. Dr. Klein said that mortality and morbidity were very high among the slaves. Following his claim Dr. Klein asked a pertinent question which he himself failed to answer. "What were the macroeconomic consequence of the slave trade on Africa.?" Dr. Klein thesis that Africa had an established slave market that even resisted the abolition movement and abolition does not hold much worthwhile thinking. The reiteration is worthwhile. What is the sociological and psychological impact of the slave trade on Africa today? However, his additional questions are helpful Dr. Klein asked. Did the goods purchased with slaves add to or detract from African economic development, actual and potential, and, second, what was the demographic impact of the loss of such a large population, both in local and continental terms? The Sociologist is to be relied upon here and the Social Anthropologist is equally required here. However, Dr. Walter Rodney has partly answered these questions for us. Dr. Rodney claimed that a major part of Africa's under-development lies in the historical fact that the slave trade extracted not the aged and infirmed but the fittest of the young men and women. The barracoons on the plantations is good attestations. Likewise, biblically in the first and second great Exiles of the Covenant people, it was the fittest, the professionals and educated that were exiled. Paradoxically in the return of the exiles to rebuild the Temple the mission was successful because the said professionals, fittest and educated returned to rebuild the Temple. Africa is not like the biblical exiles. African slaves were left deeply wounded psychologically and with permanent economical dis-empowerment. Slaves were kept by the churches in a state of permanent ignorance for physical and psychological control. The degree of dis-empowerment is to be seen and evaluated in the realm of stultification, suboptimization, dramatizations, psychological dependence, destitution, intellectual redundancy and general dis-empowerment politically because the slaves were not kept during slavery as a consolidated community. Demographical randomizations was a strategy and programme.

The Berlin Conference of 1884-85 that separated the continent of Africa and the transatlantic slave trade of 500 years have impacted beyond current estimation and acknowledgement sociologically and psychologically on Africa. Pan-Africanism and the Diasporas are a significant beginning for restoration and development. Prof. Seymour Drescher in his 2009 publication “Abolition” A History of Slavery and Antislavery says. “The first international conference on Africa met in Berlin in 1884-85. Its primary purpose was to formalize the process of determining the boundaries of domination not emancipation. The creation of a new German overseas empire and the simultaneous acceleration of French military ambition in Africa were clear signs that the era of undisputed British paramountcy beyond Europe was over.” Dr. Drescher goes on to say that” With the convening of the Berlin conference, the British press noted that the terms of power had clearly shifted towards a multipolar rather than a British hegemonic context.”

Chapter 26
Haiti - A Symbol of Dis-empowerment

A remarkable and significant feature of European and British Historiography is the detailed records kept of the transatlantic slave trade. Dr. Nicholas Draper thesis is a good example. The Price of Emancipation. Slave-ownership, compensation and British Society at the End of Slavery. Whilst the records are outstandingly detailed, various attempts had been made deliberately by white historians and particularly by the major Churches for Africans and the Diasporas educationally not to be properly informed of their history. Dr. Seymour Drescher has given us one important reason. He says that "Slavery had become such an embarrassment in the Western lexicon that it presented obstacles to gradual legislative elimination: De-legalization seemed the safest, cheapest, and least disruptive strategy." If I were to pose a question to 100 African- Caribbean adults for them to name 25 English persons that were involved in the flagitious enslavement history of black people. I am confident that they would perhaps begin with Queen Elizabeth, William Wilberforce, Thomas Buxton, Christopher Columbus, John Wesley, Sir. John Hawkins, Rev. John Newton (Amazing Grace) No black person should sign this song- if they knew their history). etc. Provocatively should I turned the question the other way. Name me not a 100 but 10 distinguished black persons who were involved in the transatlantic slave trade. I am equally confident that they would not know the names of Ignatius Sancho, Harriet Jacobs, Frederick Douglas, Toussaint L'Ouverture, Olaudah Equiano, Sam Sharp, Quamina, Nanny, Tacky, Cudjoe or Paul Bogle, Quobna Ottoban Cugoano (he was the first African slave to demand total abolition of slave trade and emancipation of slaves). Education is power. Education is empowerment. Education is a dynamic tool. It is partly for this reason that the major churches perpetuated a programme of keeping the slaves in a state of permanent ignorance. At the end of slavery not the so-called mythical abolition of Slavery in 1807. Rather in the 1830's. The slaves were awarded with the reiteration legacies of Ignorance, Destitution and permanent powerlessness. Two hundred years later the majority of Africa and African-descendants are still at the same anthropological station of dis-empowerment, alienation and dis-connection, dysfunctionalism and paralysis.

We are poignantly reminded by the immortal C.L.R. James that at his arrival in Britain he was unable to find any information of serious importance on the San Domingo Revolution under the prodigious leadership of Toussaint L'Ouverture. He had to travel to France for his 'indagation' research. Most white historians only mentioned Hayti (Haiti) in flippant passing without any serious academic consideration or laudation. But William Wilberforce is elevated and laudated comprehensively. Again, Dr. Drescher help is appreciated under his chapter- Reversion in Europe "The centenary of British colonial slave emancipation in 1933, was celebrated as a national and imperial triumph. The city of Hull, the home town of Wilberforce, was the designated site of celebration. A great civic procession led by Hull's Lord Mayor and a host of dignitaries and descendants of the liberator filed past his birthplace, his grammar school, and its assembled students. The Archbishop of York consecrated the proceedings, accompanied by hymns and spirituals of black and white choruses. The flags of fifty nations were simultaneous unfurled before tens of thousands of spectators."

C. L .R .James illuminating thesis in his "A History of Negro Revolt" made the point very perspicuous in the account of the Haitian Revolution led by Toussaint L'Ouverture, Rigaud and Victor Hugues. "The British and the Americans, themselves the greatest slave-holders in the world, were all for the victory of the blacks in order to drive out the French. All through Leclerc's campaign the British and American newspapers cursed the French and praised Toussaint and the blacks." And C. L. R. James was equally forceful and dogmatic when he said "The success of the San Domingo blacks killed the West Indian slave-trade and slavery. France hoped for many years that she would regain the colony. The Haytians let her know that they would resist to the last man and burn everything to the ground. France therefore resigned herself to the loss and with the removal of San Domingo from the West Indian trade, abolition of the slave-trade in 1807 and of slavery in 1833 followed."

We are aware of the British and the American double-standard and perfidiousness towards Haiti as the first black republic. The symbol of black liberation and black power. America turned tail, 'I supported France in her repugnant rape of Haiti'. Prof. Hilary Beckles from the University of the West-Indies on 24th January 2010 wrote this timely and relevant article entitled "The hate and the quake."

The University of the West Indies in the process of conceiving how best to deliver a major conference on the theme 'Rethinking And Rebuilding Haiti.' I am very keen to provide an input into this exercise because for too long there has been a popular perception that somehow the Haitian nation-building project, launched on January 1, 1804, has failed on account of mismanagement, ineptitude, corruption.

Buried beneath the rubble of imperial propaganda, out of both Western Europe and the United States, is the evidence which shows that Haiti's independence was defeated by an aggressive North-Atlantic alliance that could not imagine their world inhabited by a free regime of Africans as representatives of the newly emerging democracy.

The evidence is striking, especially in the context of France. The Haitians fought for their freedom and won, as did the Americans fifty years earlier. The Americans declared their independence and crafted an extraordinary constitution that set out a clear message about the value of humanity and the right to freedom, justice and liberty.

In the midst of this brilliant discourse, they chose to retain slavery as the basis of the new nation state. The founding fathers therefore could not see beyond race, as the free state was built on a slavery foundation. The water was poisoned in the well; the Americans went back to the battlefield a century later to resolve the fact that slavery and freedom could not comfortably co-exist in the same place.

The French, also, declared freedom, fraternity and equality as the new philosophies of their national transformation and gave the modern world a tremendous progressive boost by doing so. They abolished slavery, but Napoleon Bonaparte could not imagine the republic without slavery and targeted the Haitians for a new, more intense regime of slavery. The

British agreed, as did the Dutch, Spanish and Portuguese. All were linked in communion over the 500 000 Blacks in Haiti, the most populous and prosperous Caribbean colony. As the jewel of the Caribbean, they all wanted to keep their hands on it. With a massive slave base, the English, French and Dutch salivated over owning it- and the people

The people won a ten-year war, the bloodiest in history, and declared their independence. Every other country in the Americas was based on slavery. Haiti was freedom, and proceeded to place in its 1805 Independence Constitution that any person of African descent who arrived on its shores would be declared free, and a citizen of the republic. For the first time since slavery had commenced, Blacks were the subjects of mass freedom and citizenship in a nation.

The French refused to recognise Haiti's independence and declared it an illegal parish state. The Americans, whom the Haitians looked to in solidarity as their mentor in independence, refused to recognize them, and offered solidarity instead to the French. The British, who were negotiating with the French to obtain the ownership title to Haiti, also moved in solidarity, as did every other nation-state the Western world.

Haiti was isolated at birth. It was ostracised and denied access to world trade, finance, and institutional development. It was the most vicious example of national strangulation recorded in modern history.

The Cubans, at least, have had Russia, China, and Vietnam. The Haitians were alone from inception. The crumbling began. Then came 1825; the moment of full truth. The republic is celebrating its 21st anniversary. There is national euphoria in the streets of Port-au-Prince.

The economy is bankrupt; the political leadership isolated. The cabinet took the decision that the state of affairs could not continue. The country had to find a way to be inserted back into the world economy. The French government was invited to a summit. Officials arrived and told the Haitian government that they were willing to recognize the country as a sovereign nation but it would have to pay compensation and reparation in exchange. The Haitians, with backs to the wall, agreed to pay the French. The French government sent a team of accountants and actuaries into Haiti in order to place a value on all lands, all physical assets, the 500 000 citizens were formerly enslaved, animals, and all other commercial properties and services. The sums amounted to 150 million gold francs. Haiti was told to pay this reparation to France in return for national recognition."

Haiti's economical, political and social disempowerment was deliberately and immorally created. For over two hundred years no French President ever set foot on Haitian soil. In February 2010 the French President visited Haiti with a promise of 400.000.000 dollars towards their Earthquake recovery programme. Castigation is morally and politically right for France, but we should not forget the ambiguous programmes and plots of the British and the Americans in particular. Haiti's dis-empowerment economically and politically is basically due to the culture of Racism. Africa needs to take a very close look at the Haitian situation both historically and existentially.

Paternalism and Schweitzeristic charity is not empowerment and liberation. The USA CNN is very conspicuous in Haiti. Haiti played an historical function in securing America from France. Next Haiti is geographically and demographically on the door steps of the USA. It is atonement and the quest for forgiveness? The Haitian must make sure they are in the driving seat. They must take fully and accountable responsibility. They must retain the reality of their blood, tears and sweat freedom. That freedom was the illumination of the Caribbean region. It was the inspiration for the Marcus Garvey movement and philosophy. The January 2010 earthquake must not be seen in apocalyptic terms but rather a wake-up call for greater accountability and responsibility. How many black counties including Africa stood shoulder to shoulder with Haiti? There is an exigent need for Africa and the Diasporas to begin with a massive mobilization of a Moral Crusade against the USA, Europe and Britain. This is well overdue. The starting post is collective-consciousness-connection.

What of the black men and women who through their rebellions and revolutions precipitated and dictated the time table and chronology for abolition and emancipation of racial slavery.

We have seen from the account of Dr, Seymour Drescher, the British vacuous celebration and elevation of William Wilberforce whom Dr. Eric Williams rightly placed laconically to foot-notes. In this thesis Wilberforce would be space dissipation. The power and recalcitration of slave men and women has been widely ignored by white historians. It is a traditional characteristic of Europeans and British in their joint endeavours to secure within their racial systems the concealment of the historical truths from black people. The purpose is for the continuation of backwardness and dis-empowerment. Nevertheless the historical records are well premised for black scholars to make known the characters and personalities of those audacious black slave trade men and women who died for their ontological freedom. Their ontological freedom was denied them by European and British Christianity which culturally and theologically saw no incongruity between the enslavement of Africans based on Racism and their cultural God and Christianity.

Prof. Roger Anstey coined the phrase in describing the transatlantic slave trade as a (Dynamic System) without fully explaining or delineating full understanding of the conundrum and the fundamental economic source that slavery was to the economic foundation of Europe and Britain. Britain it must be said placated and pretended in a small measure of desire for the ending of the slave trade. This was so, in the form of gradual abolition and gradual emancipation. The French and German saw their trick and deception at the Berlin Conference in 1884-85 and declared the immediate termination of the transatlantic slave trade. Out of this deception, reiteration is necessary that it was the black slaves who reassembled the game and in that process dictated the termination of the slave trade. Toussaint's contribution cannot be overstated in changing the land-designation of West Indian slave trade. Procrastination was the administrative card-game of the British. But the ontological will of the slaves changed the terms and conditions of the game- which the British failed to acknowledged.

Chapter 27
Summation

The improvident conditions of Africa and African-descendants has been a great concern in my theological thinking and Liberation Theology postulations and the historical currents that created the conditions of dysfunctionalism and paralysis among Africans and the Diasporas. Dr. Richard Hart astutely reminded us that of all the races on earth the black race is the door-mat of society. Prof. James Cone (African-American theologian) in a similar vane said that the black race is always at the bottom in society. Sociologically, economically, technologically and scientifically. Africa according to the transatlantic slave trade history had been the economic foundation of Europe, Britain and the United States. The transatlantic slave trade of 500 years have left the black race powerless and backward this was the philosophy and programme of the dynamic institution of slavery. Black powerlessness and backwardness was the racial cultural philosophy and economic programme deliberately pre-planned by the royals, governments, merchants, enslavers and the major denominations. The Anglican Church confidently through its Archbishops, Bishops and ordained ministers even called for a specific "International Conference" to discuss the "Theological Justification" of the transatlantic (Black-African) slave trade in the name of Almighty God- European Christianity and Jesus Christ.

In this paper based on forensic hermeneutic indagation principles, I have looked critically at the relationship of dis-empowerment and engagement historically in conjunction with the impacts of the reiteration legacies of the transatlantic slave trade. I was motivated by the gravity of the historiographical literatures and published works on Slavery. I have examined the various traumatic syndromes suffered by the slaves and the impact on Africa and African-descendants today. Some traumatic syndromes are destructive to the core and bones. I had to unearth these as Dr. NA 'Im Akbar (Breaking the Chains of Psychological Slavery) and DR. Joy Leary (Post Traumatic Slave Syndrome) have articulated in their books with amazing illumination and contextualization.

A significant area of my thesis is in oscillation between Dis-empowerment-Engagement- Reparation-Pan-Africanism and the optative optimism to see Africa and the Diaspora with respectful recognition on the world stage. One way of getting to this stage is through scientific and technological powers. African- political-unification through the philosophy of Pan-Africanism would be just as effective. African-political unification is very necessary as a dynamic oppugnation (opposition) to European and British hegemony over Africa. On the other-hand it cannot be forgotten, that Africa and the Diasporas have 500 years of oppression, exploitation, brain-washing by the churches, theological and doctrinal inculcation of stultification to overcome. In addition the reiteration transatlantic legacies are still permeating the lives and minds of African-descendants today.

Mr. Robin Walker and Mr. C.LR. James have shown that African-descendants historically had been positive and powerful. I have emulated both scholars by looking at the great struggles of a number of slave men and women that many white scholars have not paid any attention or appreciation to them for their tremendous contributions. Memorialisation of the 'kebuka' ancestors and their unique places in black history are important. The crimes of European and British is voluminous. One such flagitious crime is their deliberate policy and philosophy to negate, obliterate, fragment and lampoon black history. Marcus Garvey looked at the slaves labouring on the cotton plantation in America and he reminded the slaves with these words "Stand up you mighty race." Slavery has robbed and excorticated the black race of our greatness. It is in this sphere that disempowerment especially psychologically is entombed in the psyche of black people.

It is common practice and expectation whenever Reparation is topically part of a conversation to see reparation purely as economic redress for the worst crime ever committed against a race of people. There is no parallel in history to the transatlantic slave trade of 500 years of racial brutality by Europeans, British and Americans based on Racism. It was enmeshed in theology and philosophy of religion. I consciously called on black scholars, black church leaders and academics to begin with a new and radical hermeneutics of theology, history, sociology, economics and philosophy of religion. The oppressors morally have no logical apologetics. White theology and philosophy of religion are based on oppression and the transatlantic slave trade mentality and culture of superiority, political and economical hegemony. It is grossly opprobrious to that which the slaves had in abundance (human decency). It is necessary to point out the opprobrium of the transatlantic slave trade which was enshrined in European and British theology of Infralapsarianism. It was based on and practiced as such without any moral content.

I have made the sharp distinction between political reparation and ecclesial reparation. Historians and theologians cannot separate the political from the denominational reparations. The churches and political hegemony were one and the same. Remove the function of the churches and slavery would have died before it begun. Slavery was made possible and pandemic because the churches rapidly disseminated a cultural and semantical Christianity of oppression and exploitation. It was indeed a flagitious form of Christianity without any moral content and integrity. Hence, the urgent 'Reparation Programme' and movement must be combined. This is a challenge especially to black politicians, black political leaders of Black countries. Black Theologians and particularly Black Churches within Africa and on the global spheres.

My admission in writing this paper is that academic justice to the subject of Dis-empowerment and Engagement cannot be done purely by studying the monographic and historiographical records and Literatures. The Psychological and Sociological Impact of the transatlantic (Black African) slave trade on Africa and the Diasporas is highly imperative. This therefore is a deficiency. However, my ambition is to put this matter right with my next paper on (The Psychological and Sociological Impact of Slavery on Africa 500years). This research will take me physically to Africa- perhaps to the University of Legeon Ghana West Africa. My Country of Study will be Ghana seeing that Ghana was the major Slave Trading Country in Africa.

My forensic hermeneutic 'eximious indagation' research was done without any academic aid or supervision. I therefore take full responsibility for the paragraphically contents of this innovative groundbreaking paper.

Many areas need further investigations and research. But I often tell my students that my task is not to give them the answers but rather to provoke them to think independently theologically and historically. I hope I have done this to my readers. I have shown and given you the materials, the critical approach to hermeneutic. Theological and historical reflections. It is now your task to build on my foundation and beyond.

Robinson A. Milwood. London. July 2010

Bibliography

Thavolia Glymph. Out of the House of Bondage- The Transformation of The Plantation Household. Pub. By Cambridge University Press.2008

Nicholas Draper. The Price of Emancipation- Slave-Ownership, Compensation and British Society at the End of Slavery. Pub. By Cambridge University Press 2009.

Ann C. Bailey. African Voices of the Atlantic Slave Trade- Beyond the Silence and the Shame. Pub.By Beacon Press Boston 2005

William St Clair. The Grand Slave Emporium- Cape Coast Castle and British Slave Trade. Pub. BY Profile Books Ltd. 2006

S.K.B. Asante, FGA. Pan-Africanism and Regionalism. The J.B. Danquah Memorial Lecture Series 40 March 2007

W.E.B. Du Boris. The Souls of Black Folk. Pub. By Dover Publications, INC New York 1994

Nigel Sadler. The Slave Trade. Pub. By Shire Publications 2009

John Thornton. Africa and the Africans in the Making of the Atlantic

World, 1400-1800. Pub. By Cambridge University Press 2008.

Runoko Rashidi Travel Notes The Global African Community. Pub.By Runoko Rashidi 2005

C.L.R. James A History of Negro Revolt. Pub. By Frontline Books USA 2004

Gail Cameron and Stan Crooke. Liverpool Capital of the Slave Trade. Pub. By Picton Press Liverpool 1992.

Anthony Tibbles. Transatlantic Slavery. Against Human Dignity. Pub. By National Museums Liverpool. Pub.By National Museums Liverpool. 1994

Shlomo Sand. The Invention of the Jewish People. Pub. By Verso. 2009

Diarmaid MacCulloch. A History of Christianity. Pub. By Allen Lane 2009

Trading Souls. Europe's Transatlantic Trade in Africans. By. Verene A. Shepherd- Hilary McD.

Beckles. Pub. By Ian Randle Publishers Limited 2000

Hilary McD Beckles- Verene A. Shepherd. Saving Souls. The Struggle to End The Transatlkantic Trade in Africans. Pub. By. Ian Randle Publishing Limited 2007

Sian Rees. Sweet Water and Bitter- The Ships that Stopped the Slave Trade. Pub. By Chatto & Windus London 2009

Barrie Wilson. How Jesus Became Christian. The Early Christians and the Transformation of a Jewish Teacher into the Son of God. Pub. By Weidenfeld & Nicoloson. 2009

Tony Martin. The Pan-African Connection- From Slavery to Garvey and Beyond. Pub. By The Majority Press 1984

Richard Dawkins. The God Delusion. Pub. By Black Swan 2006

Lawrence A. Peskin. Captives and Countrymen- Barbary Slavery and the American Public, 1785-1816. Pub. By The Johns Hopkins University Press. 2009.

Robert E. Bonner. Mastering America- Southern Slaveholders and the Crisis of American Nationhood. Pub. By Cambridge University Press 2009.

David Beck Ryden. West Indian Slavery and British Abolition, 1783-1807. Pub. By. Cambridge University Press. 2009.

David Brion Davis. The Problem of Slavery in Western Culture. Pub. By Oxford University Press. 1996.

David Brion Davis. Inhuman Bondage. The Rise and Fall of Slavery in the New World. Pub. By Oxford University Press.2006

David Brion Davis. The Problem of Slavery in the Age of Revolution

1770-1823. Pub. By Oxford University Press. 1999.

David Brion Davis. In the Image of God. Religion, Moral Values and Our Heritage of Slavery. Pub. By. Yale University Press 2001

Steven M. Wise. Though The Heavens May Fall. The Landmark Trial That Led To The End of Human Slavery. Pub. By Pimlico 2006

Roger Anstey and P.E.H. Hair. Liverpool, the African Slave Trade and Abolition, Pub. By Historic Society of Lancashire and Cheshire. 2089.

David Richardson, Suzanne Schwarz and Anthony Tibbles. Liverpool and Transatlantic Slavery. Pub.By Liverpool University Press 2007.

Stanley Engrerman, Seymour Drecher and Robert Paquette. Slavery. Pub. By.Oxford University Press. 2001

David Babydeen, John Gilmore ND Cecily Jones. The Oxford Companion to Black British History.
Pub. By. Oxford University Press. 2008.

Harriet Jacobs- Incidents in the Life of a Slave Girl Written by Herself. Pub. By Penguin-Books. 2000.

M.K. Gandhi- An Autobiography or The Story of My Experiment With Truth. Pub. By Penguin Books 2007

David Pawson Unlocking the Bible. Pub. By Collins 2007

William Henry Foster. Gender, Mastery and Slavery. From European to Atlantic World Frontiers. Pub. By Palgrave Macmillan- Ann Taylor Allen. 2007

Rebecca J. Scott. Degrees of Freedom. Pub. By Harvard University Press. 2005

Charles Freeman- A New History of Early Christianity. Pub. By. Yale University Press. 200

Alister E. McGrath. The Christian Theology Reader Third Edition. Pub. By. Blackwell. 2007.

Paul E. Lovejoy. Identity in the Shadow of Slavery. Pub. By Continum 200,

Seymour Drescher. Abolition. A History of Slavery and Antislavery. Pub. By Cambridge University
Press. 2009.

Karen Armstrong A History of God. Pub. By. William Heinemann Ltd.1993

Richard Hart. . Slaves Who Abolished Slavery. Volume 1 and 2. Pub. By. University of the West Indies. 1080

Gad Heuman. The Killing Time. The Morant Bay Rebellion in Jamaica. Warwick University Caribbean Studies. Pub. By. Macmillan Caaambridge.1994

Frederick Douglas. MY Bondage and My Freedom. Pub. By. Penguin

Mwalimu K. Bommani Baruti(Kebuka) (Remembering the Middle Passage) Pub. By. Morris Publishing 2005,

Moses D. E. Nwulia: Britain and Slavery in East Africa. Pub. By Three Continents Press. 1974

Eric Williams : Capitalism and Slavery. Pub. By. Andre Deutsch. 1943

Ronald Segal : The Black Diaspora Pub. By. Faber and Faber London. 1995

Vincent Harding: There is A River- The Black Struggle for Freedom in America. Pub. By. Harcourt Brace Jovanovich New York. 1981.

Robin Walker: When We Ruled. Pub. By Every Generation Media. 2006

Helen Thomas. Romanticism and Slave Narratives- Transatlantic Testimonies. Pub.By. Cambridge University Press.

Srividhya Swaminathan: Debating The Slave Trade. Rhetoric of British National Identity, 1759-1815.
Pub.By.Ashgate. 2009.

Elizabeth Abbott: Sugar. A Bittersweet History. Pub. By. Duckworth Overlook. 2009.

End Notes

To all Africans and African-descendants throughout the Diasporas, it must be remembered that the slaves suffered injustice and indignity. They were reduced to the level of chattle by legal and theological definitions, because of Racism, Economic avariciousness, without any moral or religious integrity and perspective. The transgression of the Holy God- A God not of any one race but the God of all races because God is the Absolute Creator. Redemption is available for the enslaved and the enslavers. The Merchants, the Politicians, the Theologians and Philosophers. The slaves experienced subjugation and stripped of their humanity: The slaves never cried or called for imprecation on their enslavers but rather for mercy and forgiveness. There is a lot to be remembered but we the descendants must never forget that the great and noble ancestors persevered to see Abolition of the Slave Trade in Africans and the Abolition of Slavery and Emancipation Day. It was a Day they fought and rebelled for. Shalom.

Physiological-psychological-spiritual-cultural-sociological-economical and theological dis-empowerment of Black people, i.e. Africans through Expropriation and Enslavement. Thereby- the creation of the reiteration legacy of permanent dis-empowerment and improvidence of Black people.

Slaves vilification and intellectual vacuity.

1) The sodomnization of men, women and children by the churches.
2) Baracoonism-forceful breeding of slave children for economic rapacity.
3) Dungeonism. Forceful imprisonment of slaves underground.
4) Men, women and children were used for target practice by shooting the head off.
5) Mutiliantion of the body, especially slave women who refused the sexual advancement of the slave traders and enslavers.
6)Random gang-rape of men, women and children.
7)Public rape of women on the plantation.
8)Organized rape by enslavers, friends, merchants, traders and missionaries.
9) Trained blood-hound dogs stripped the flesh from the bones of slaves who ran-away.
10) The sole of slaves feet were cut off with razor for being disobedient.
11) The hanging of women slaves by one leg naked for refusing sexual advances of the slave master.
12) Women slaves were hanged on a tree limb and slowly cut into pieces with a sword for refusing sex with the slave master.
13) Breaking of the neck of children was a fun game and sport.
14) Bashing the brain of children was a sport.
15) Pregnant women were placed over a pit and whipped for refusing to carry her pregnany.
16) Persistent beating/whipping of slaves in order to delineate the slave master's power.
17) Slave women were hanged naked on a tree limb to be eaten by the crows.

18) Deffication in the mouth of slaves for running away and with their mouth tied for upto six hours.
19) Ampituation of limbs for small wrongs.
20) Dumping of slaves into the sea alive for the sharks to eat.
21) Men were forced to watched the rape of wives, Daughters, Girlfriends, Sisters and Mothers.
22) Public execution of slaves to instill fear.
23) Brutal whipping of slaves at the whipping post until the bood turned into a ruinning stream.
24) Men were forced to stripped naked their mother and whipped her to death, likewise girlfriends.
25) Slaves were fed alive to lions and tigers.
26) Dis-emboweling of slaves was a common practice.
27) Slaves were placed in the room/ door of NO Return for being disobedient.
28) Slaves were sold at the emporium (market place) like chattle.
29) Slaves were taught to believed that they were inherently inferior to white-people. This became a doctrine in the Methodist Church.
30) Slaves were taught to hate each other. Showed disrespect to each other and never to be united.
31) Slaves were kept in perpetual ignorance in order to create powerlessness.

These horrendous and henious crimes were committed to the Black race by the Archbishops, Bishops, Ministers and Missionaries in the name of a white God, Semantical cultural Christianity and a white Jesus Christ.

With the combination of 500 years of Slavery and the Maafa of 300,000.000. Africans without reparation to Africa from Europe, Britain and the USA. The calamity of dictatorship by strongmen, corruption, civil wars, genocide, widespread poverty and the interventions and manipulation of Africa by Western powers had relegated Africa to the position of an aid "basket case," the world's poorest and least developed Continent. R.A.M.

Lightning Source UK Ltd.
Milton Keynes UK
10 October 2010

161034UK00001B/2/P